The Happy Hoo-Ha

By: M. E. Nesser

This book is dedicated to Mark:
the man *behind* my hoo-ha.

A special thank you to Cathy & David
for supporting my hoo-ha.

TABLE OF CONTENTS

Panties Off, Please   1

Are Bald Beavers Better?   5

Just Another Bartender   15

The Vagina, a.k.a...   19

What's That Smell?   25

Guys Are the Real Pussies   41

So What Kind of Woman Waxes It All?   53

Bald at Any Age   63

Mastering a Woman's Mound   71

Crazy Shit People Tell Me   87

Now He Can Lick Me...   113

Panties Off, Please

"**S**lacks and panties off, and I'll have you bald in five." That's how I greet almost every new client that walks into the salon. It's my casual, no nonsense approach to what I do for a living.

So are you thinking about getting a Brazilian? You know...the type of waxing service that removes all of your pubic and rectal hair? Then I am here to set the record straight on the subject. By some bizarre twist of fate, I have become an extraordinarily busy Brazilian wax technician. It's an interesting profession, wouldn't you say? I have waxed thousands of women and have seen and heard just about everything. If you aren't sure about getting one, you still may be interested in the logistics of the procedure. What goes on in the confines of a private wax room will amuse and amaze you. This is definitely a trend that is sweeping the globe, and I totally understand why people are fascinated by the entire experience. There are naked women in a room together and what goes on includes some pain, embarrassment, and usually some outrageous conversation. If you're a voyeur who is fascinated with the female anatomy, I hope I can satisfy you in some fucked-up way. If you are some kind of sexual deviant that is obsessed with the notion of hot wax, women, and pain, I feel pretty confident that you'll enjoy a lot of what I have to say. And if you are simply a woman who is interested in getting a Brazilian, then it is a pleasure to meet you. Regardless of your interest in the procedure that leads to a beautifully bald beaver, I am here to help make it a more positive experience, not only for the person thinking about getting it done but also the technician performing the service. I am also here to amuse and potentially shock people who just cannot fathom why someone would choose this as a profession, and why anyone in their right mind would have this done. In the past sixteen years, I have become an expert in this field and there are a lot of do's and don'ts that need discussing before you venture into the land of the perfectly primped pussy.

My job is even more interesting because I work with my husband, Mark. Although he'd love to do Brazilians, I think it's a lawsuit just waiting to happen. It's tough to not touch a woman inappropriately when your hands are between her legs and everything is sticky. I actually had one of my fingers slide inside a woman recently, which was a very strange sensation. It was also a first for me. I'm glad I had gloves on. When I told Mark that I wanted to write a book, I don't think he realized how much I had to say on the subject. Believe me, the pussy is a very interesting topic and I love talking about it. His only advice since I started this project was to "make sure it grabs the reader by the balls." No problem, babe! I've got a pretty crazy story to tell and there will be some ball-grabbing going on.

If you come to see me as a client, I don't care what kind of personality you have...shy, outgoing, passive, aggressive...or what kind of body you have...trim, large, soft, muscular. I think all women have some kind of attractive characteristics about them. It is this kind of thinking that makes it much easier to work on as many women as I do each week. I can honestly say that I am able to find something enjoyable about each person who walks into our salon. When you have your hands between someone's legs and are spreading their lips apart, they are more prone to tell you intimacies that they may never tell another soul. The best advice I can give anyone going into the beauty business is to be open-minded. (Having a strong stomach isn't a bad idea either.) The more outrageous the story, the more I enjoy my day. Everybody needs someone to share crazy stories with or ask embarrassing questions to, and I seem to be that girl. No question is too shocking and no confession seems too off-the-wall. A girl turns on her side, lifts up her cheek so I can wax her rectal area, and admits that she just did it in the ass for the first time and really liked it. Chalk it up to another good day.

Are Bald Beavers Better?

"Now it smells better down there." When a three-hundred-pound woman exclaims that this is the best part of getting a Brazilian, then what can I say? Every woman has her own reason. Hair can generate heat and moisture to the area it is covering, especially when confined in clothing. And if the person is overweight or unwell and has difficulty cleansing her parts properly, then the discomfort of getting waxed is even more worth her while. So hygiene is definitely a contributing factor to the compulsion to be bald. And I guess if it can rip away some nasty odor, there's a bonus.

It is kind of a strange new trend, having no pubic or rectal hair. Don't think I am complaining, because it has changed my life. And I have loved almost every minute of it. But it is an interesting phenomenon that all of a sudden having pubic hair is a bad thing. My teens tell me that boys and girls alike are shaving it all off. So if you are one of the few people that has hair between your legs, then you must wonder what is this obsession with being bald? I definitely have my theories on the subject and would like to share them with those who cannot imagine why anybody would put themselves through the torture of having a stranger put hot wax on their genitalia then rip it off in a seemingly harsh and barbaric manner. And, for others, it is fascinating to speculate why men and women feel compelled to look like toddlers.

So is the look of a prepubescent girl really sexy or are we, as women, just a little paranoid about feeling cleaner? Or are we, as a society, just obsessed with germs and hygiene in general? One of my clients told me that she constantly asks her husband if it smells okay down there. He told her that sometimes he wished there was a little natural smell, but there never is. She's a regular client who maintains her completely hair-free hoo-ha on a monthly basis. She also is obsessed with keeping it clean inside and out. She told me about a girl she knew in high school. She said she could smell this girl's pussy even when the girl was dressed. It was one of those gross memories that has always kind of haunted her. Knowing that it was possible to smell her lady parts from afar has made her more conscientious than ever in her efforts to keep herself odor-free.

Nevertheless, I think we are getting a little neurotic about germs. Anti-bacterial soaps, hand sanitizers, and deodorizing sprays...sometimes I find it all baffling. I'm not saying that I want a client to come into the salon for a wax who is unclean, but what is happening in our society is that we can't even leave home without a travel-size hand sanitizer? We are working so hard to de-germ our environment and our bodies but people aren't getting healthier; they are getting sicker. So my epiphany about this topic is that we should re-examine where we focus our compulsive behavior. How about we laugh a little more and have a lot more sex?

Let's get back to the bush. I offer many options to my clients when they come in for their first Brazilian. Not every woman is comfortable with a completely hair-free area. A lot of women prefer to leave some hair in the front so they do not look like their seven-year-old daughters. One of my clients named that look a Brazini, a cross between a bikini and a Brazilian. Looks like a bikini from the front but it's a celebration of hairlessness down below. This woman happened to be in her fifties when she coined this phrase for me, which reinforces the fact that any age can benefit from this service. And I hope she feels proud that she discovered a pretty cool name for one of our most popular services at the salon.

Many women come to an appointment simply desiring a bikini wax. Often their main objection to a Brazilian is the anticipated pain. Yet, for most women, it is the sides of the bikini area and the top that are the most painful to have waxed. Trust me when I tell you that your labia and rectal area are a lot tougher than you think. So, in most cases, I strongly encourage going all the way.

Women are not alone in their unease with a totally hair-free zone. There are men who feel uncomfortable when their women are totally bald as well. Many of my clients have told me that their partners feel like a pedophile when they engage in sexual relations with a bald woman. For many men, the hair is sexy and represents a more desirable, womanly body. We appreciate the guys wanting to be able to distinguish between the females in the household. I'd hate to think my husband likes me bald because it reminds him of our four-year-old daughter. In fact, I think most women are quite comfortable with that reasoning. It's also reassuring to hear that there are men out there adding their input about our grooming habits. A woman appreciates any interest a man shows in her as well as her parts. But I do think it is important for the woman to feel comfortable with her own body, and that is my primary focus.

No matter what style you want to see down there, I am here to please. It doesn't matter one way or another to me. I will wax as much or as little as desired. Many women I have met like to keep a little hair covering the hood of their genitalia because the sensation is too intense when it is all exposed. Now, take just a second to think about what I just said. Having no hair over the clitoris can make it almost too sensitive. Who would have thunk it? So if you are a woman who needs a little help getting aroused, maybe a little hair removal is just what the doctor ordered.

With regard to feelings down there, many women have confided to me that having no hair has increased their sexual sensations and made their love-making much more intense. You're welcome! In this age of anti-depressants and anti-anxiety medicines that can take away your sexual feelings, women are desperate for anything that can help jump-start their libido. I have also found that women going through any part of menopause have found their sex drive waning as well. From what I understand, during that phase of maturity, the vagina tends to dry out. This can actually make the skin more sensitive to being waxed Note to self!!).More importantly, the vagina can be uncooperative and unresponsive. This is definitely not a change in the body that women eagerly anticipate. Many dread it. I truly believe that giving an older woman a Brazilian can be beneficial. If being bald can boost your confidence, make you feel a little daring, and allow the clit to be more exposed so it has more feeling, then women should have started getting rid of their pubic hair a long time ago. And maybe they were, but they just weren't talking about it. It still baffles me how our society now openly talks about everything. But it delights me as well, because now it allows me to talk about a subject near to my heart: hairy hoo-ha's.

When I look back and think about how life was when I first started doing Brazilians at the salon, these were definitely hush-hush services that weren't talked about openly. Now the talk is everywhere: on television, in magazines and books. In fact, we have a banner on the front of our salon that says "Home of the Brazilian Wax." Mark thought it was important for the public to know how we have dedicated our lives to making women happier, so he had a banner made to advertise our dedication to this service. Since I started writing this book four years ago, we have updated the banner. It now says "Home of the 10-Minute Brazilian."

I'll never forget the first call we ever got requesting a Brazilian. Mark answered the phone. He covered the mouth piece and said, "Honey, do you do Brazilians?" I said, "Yes." He asked me, "On whom?" I responded, "I can't tell you!" He wanted to know if I charged more. I told him that I didn't. He thought we probably should since it took more time. I didn't know. The women I did Brazilians on were my guinea pigs with this service and I appreciated them letting me practice on them. So we added ten dollars to the bikini rate, which was twenty-five dollars at the time. I remember the first girl who called was from California and her hair was so incredibly resistant. I had never had a tough one before and, after she left the salon, I wasn't sure that this was something I wanted to continue doing, because her hair was so difficult to remove. Fortunately, I got over my apprehension and have concentrated on being the best wax technician possible.

Whenever I wax someone completely bald, I include the happy trail of hair that travels to the belly button. I can't imagine why anyone would want a completely bald pubic area and leave a patch of hair under the navel. One time I had a woman with a big, bushy Afro between her legs come in to have it all waxed off. I started with the bikini line and saw that the happy trail looked like a full-fledged mustache. Without hesitation, I put a strip of wax on the area and ripped it off in one quick rip. That's when she sat up and spat threatening attitude in my face. She loved her happy trail. She actually screamed at me and said, "How dare you rip that off!" I thought she was going to hit me. She told me I had no right to remove her happy trail because she only wanted her bush gone. It was definitely my mistake. I should have asked permission first. It just never occurred to me. The rest of the service passed quietly and uncomfortably and even though I tried my hardest to appease her, I never saw her again.

Many women worry that the hair carries odor that may be displeasing to their partner. For the record, I have discussed this with many men and it seems that unless you have really poor hygiene, they love the natural smell you have between your legs. It has to do with your natural pheromones, and that is a good thing to know.

Regarding pheromones, one of my strippers told me she gets better tips when she leaves some hair between her legs. Even though her G-string covers the front where we leave the hair, she is convinced that men are attracted to her womanly scent. That is also good to know.

What I really think it comes down to is that when women have all these worries in their head, their bodies will never be completely satisfied during a romantic encounter. If the simple act of removing all the hair can give a girl just the added confidence she needs, then I am providing a worthwhile service with my less-than-ten-minute procedure. Fewer women would have to fake it, if they weren't so worried about their twat being smelly. They can just lie back, relax, and cum like a champ.

It is both unbelievable and incredibly sad all the hang-ups that women have about their bodies. Women complain to me on a daily basis about the different areas of their bodies they are unhappy with. "My ass is fat," "my muffin top could feed the homeless," "my boobs are so small I look like a boy," "the dimples on my legs look like cottage cheese," "my nose is too big," "my labia aren't smooth," "my stretch marks look like a road map," "my rectum is too dark," "my eyes are too close together," "I'm sick and tired of being fat"—the list goes on and on and is never-ending! A size zero, in my opinion, is not the most feminine and alluring of body types. Some women are naturally that size, and that is wonderful, but there seems to be too much emphasis on being underweight, and, frankly, I think our men like a little something to grab on to. As far as the other parts, I think it would be pretty creepy if we all looked the same from head to toe. So you have bigger ears than your roommate. Who gives a shit? After nearly two decades of sharing intimate experiences with thousands of women, I think all women have some beautiful quality about them that should be celebrated and cherished. Way too much energy is spent lamenting about the parts of the body that need to be altered or perfected. Give it up already!

Women really do complain about the color of their rectum, which explains why I've had some requests for rectal bleaching over the years. This has become more popular in the pornography world. What has surprised me is that all of the requests have come from regular folks. I even had a company that sold a rectal bleaching product contact me about using their product and adding the service to our menu. As it is, I spend more time staring at assholes than I would like. So, no thanks, this is one service I'll have to pass on.

I did have a client refer to her rectum as a brown starfish. I loved that description. And, believe me, on a white girl, that's what it looks like.

I have had countless women tell me that they receive a lot more oral sex when they are waxed. For many, it is the only way they can achieve an orgasm. Unfortunately, many of my clients aren't receiving this gift from their guys because they have hair between their legs. They are, however, still expected to perform that service on their men. I would like these women to tell every one of those guys to "fuck off!" because if they aren't going down there, neither are we! I'd actually like to get a hold of all those men who deny their partners oral sex and see how they like having their pubic hair covered in hot wax and yanked out by the root. The thought of it amuses the shit out of me! One lady told me that her husband never went down on her until she met me. Last year he lost his job and she called me and said they just couldn't afford for her to get waxed anymore. Although I will miss seeing her, I totally understand that it is a luxury and may not always fit in a budget. But all I could think of was the fact that his days of going down under were over.

I know many people who do not wax must wonder who is really getting the benefit of this treatment? Since this service can be excruciating for some people, do women suffer solely for their partners or spouses or do they really do it for themselves? I have learned over the years that, for the most part, my clients wax for themselves. It makes them feel better about their bodies. I have also found that most women do not keep it up for their partner unless they like it as well. It's pretty sadistic to go through this monthly ritual if you can't justify the benefits in your own mind. There are hundreds of men offering to pay for their women to come see me. There are also tons of men simply encouraging their girls to see me. Some even offer incentives. Gotta love incentives. So I guess the answer to the question is that most women only subject their privates to my specialized service because they really want it and they feel it is worth it.

A woman came in for her first Brazilian and was shocked by how much it hurt. After the first rip, she said, "This is excruciating." I said, "No, sweetie, you used the wrong 'E' word. It's exhilarating." She said quite a bit louder, "No, it's fucking excruciating!" And I replied, "No, it's fucking exhilarating!" Then she started laughing and, by that point, I was almost finished.

I have heard countless stories about the private conversations between couples that accompany this whole Brazilian thing and I just love sharing these stories. They really can be hysterical and I have found that telling a funny story can really put a woman at ease while I am about to wax them. A client of mine had not been in for several months because she was busy with work, life, etc. and just didn't make the time to come in. Her husband made an interesting comment about her new look. He told her that although he appreciated that fact that she cared about his dental health, he was really tired of flossing on a regular basis and was hoping that she would make an appointment to see me.

A group of teenage boys were hanging out in my family room. They were talking about girls. When a certain girl's name came up, they made weird faces and acted goofy. I asked them what I was missing. One of the boys mumbled something about not liking to pull hair out of his mouth. He even made the gesture of picking something out of his teeth. Then they all got really embarrassed because they made that confession loud enough for me to hear. My son told them not to worry because they could say anything in front of me. And they can. Considering my profession, it is difficult to shock me.

Many clients start out with simply a bikini wax. When I first started waxing, that was fine with me. My bikini waxes were never normal anyway, which I think added to my popularity. Whenever I gave someone a regular bikini, I would assume that at some point she would wear a thong or a G-string type of panty. In that case, there couldn't be any hair left next to the rectum or on the inside of the thigh at the very top where the leg meets the pubic area. Since my bikini waxes were so thorough, moving to the next step of removing all of the pubic hair was no big deal. In fact, in most cases, I was almost there. So when I noticed one of my girls let me wax her bikini area but she shaved the inside, I suggested we just wax the whole thing. And the rest, as they say, "is history".

When I first started waxing, one of my girls had a horrible mishap with her razor. Although she waxed the bikini line, she shaved the rest. She didn't know it was possible to wax everything down there. While trying to shave her lips, she cut herself so badly that the cut wouldn't stop bleeding. She called her gynecologist and he suggested she keep pressure on the area. So she put a maxi pad in a tight pair of underwear. After several hours, the cut wouldn't clot and she was forced to go in and have a few stitches put in to close the wound. She was very embarrassed calling the doctor for advice and then being forced to go in and have it taken care of. This was another client who decided that maybe it would be safer and a lot less embarrassing to just let me wax it all.

Logistically, shaving the pubic area can be quite complicated. The labia are soft and smushy and shaving that kind of skin can be quite challenging. Secondly, seeing the area to safely shave it can also be a feat in itself. Not everybody is that flexible and not every shower is equipped with the right apparatus for proper stepping up with one foot. And if you have any extra weight in your mid-section, forget it! There ain't no way you are going to safely get there to make it smooth and hair-free. The rectal area is even more comical to try to navigate. Without a mirror, I doubt many people can see that area. And the area surrounding your rectum is so bumpy, you have to be very careful you don't cut the skin. Rectal bleeding is never a good thing. Moral of the story...shaving can be dangerous and waxing rocks.

So, are bald beavers better? Absolutely!

Just Another Bartender

Bartender, hairdresser, wax technician...it's a crazy phenomenon how people will share their inner-most secrets to a complete stranger over a glass of beer, a haircut, or a simple bikini wax. And yet during the past twenty years in the salon, I have heard intimate details about my clients' lives that have amused, saddened, and even horrified me. It really astounds me that people are not comfortable sharing their true feelings with their own family or loved ones and feel more compelled to share things with me. Sometimes I wonder if the confessions are a type of coping mechanism.

A girlfriend told me that she is so self-conscious when she goes to the gynecologist that she has diarrhea of the mouth from the moment the doctor walks into the room. It is her way of dealing with the fact that he is going to look at her imperfect body. She said talking incessantly keeps her distracted when he crawls inside her vagina and starts feeling around and scraping tissue, which usually doesn't feel very good. So it seems to me that, in my business, it's possible that the honest disclosures are as cathartic as the actual hair removal. When a crazy confession is shared, we both win. A woman can unload any thought or emotion on me and not worry about being judged. And it makes me feel good to be able to listen and, sometimes, even offer some valid advice. So maybe I am just another bartender.

A woman entered the salon right before closing time, hoping to get a bikini and brow wax. She had been a periodic client of mine for several years but not someone I ever saw on a regular monthly basis. When we went upstairs, I could sense some awkwardness in her demeanor. I asked her what was going on and she hesitated like she was afraid to share her problem. But, at the same time, it was obvious that she needed to talk to someone. Within minutes, she told me that she moved out of her boyfriend's house and was feeling really uncomfortable about a new relationship that had evolved with a lesbian co-worker. She found this woman extremely attractive and was having inexplicable feelings toward her. She was so confused. Her parents would never accept her being a lesbian and she wasn't sure that she really was. She had always dreamed about having a husband, children, and the picket fence...you know the whole scenario. She was confused and scared but incredibly attracted to this girl. I think many of us have had a moment of sexual confusion like this in our lives. I suggested that maybe she should try out this whole girl-on-girl thing and see how it really feels. That's what a lot of us do, even if we don't like to admit it. We explore those feelings at some point during adolescence and then can safely decide which way we swing. I finished her wax as she finished her story and I could tell she felt better. It meant a lot to me to be there to listen to her.

In this industry, we tend to be an integral part of our clients' lives. A college student wanted my advice on how many dates she should go on with a fraternity brother of her ex-boyfriend before she slept with him. I think a girl needs to be careful how many guys she sleeps with from one frat house. It doesn't take many for her to adopt a "whore" status. My advice was to take her time and be discrete.

Did you know there are thousands of women out there who grow their pubic hair long on purpose? It is their way of keeping themselves from sleeping around. Some of my girls refer to it as their security blanket or their chastity belt.

I have a client who has had what I refer to as a "grown up" job for four years in the field of social work. She decided to quit her job, risk giving up her health insurance, and start working on her master's degree. For extra spending money, she found a job as a waitress at a busy downtown eatery. Now she can't decide what to do. She makes so much more money four days a week as a waitress that even when she gets her master's, she won't be making the money that she is making now. It is a difficult decision to make, especially with the cost of living continually rising. The reasonable part of your brain says, "Get a degree and work in a given field." The realistic part of the brain, however, wonders why one would bother in a field that pays so poorly when a part-time gig or a vocational occupation that doesn't require a fancy degree will lead to such a greater monetary gain. And, in my case, changing careers was the smartest move I could have ever made. It is so strange to think that I once taught first grade and now I make women look like first-graders all day long.

As a side note, let me introduce myself. My name is Mary Elizabeth, and I am a successful Brazilian wax technician. Now this is definitely not a profession that I was dreaming about when I was growing up, but it is a busy and exciting career that has brought me so much joy. The ultimate bonus is that I have been working side by side with my husband of more than twenty-five years. He does hair. I do hair removal. A match made in heaven.

I don't think anyone can truly fathom what I do all day. It can be fun, disgusting, shocking, enlightening...so much energy and emotion can be shared between two women in ten minutes that I truly feel I have earned an unofficial doctorate degree in life, relationships, and human psychology. How cool is that?

So pour me a drink and let the conversations continue...

The Vagina, a.k.a...

It continues to amuse me the pet names that women have for their most intimate parts. So I decided to start writing a list one day. You would be shocked at the nicknames some of the most pristine, conservative women call their privates. Picture this: blond, fair-skinned, Republican, mom, attorney, soft-spoken...getting the first strip pulled from the bikini line and she yells, "My fucking twat!" I know that I may not always appear sympathetic, but it was impossible not to laugh.

I had another woman who was in her fifties tell me that she felt like her snatch had been violated. I guess the act of ripping out pubic hair with hot wax can give one that impression. But, believe me, it is not my goal to violate anyone. Yet I must admit that the swearing in conjunction with the crude referrals to the vagina keep me amused on a daily basis.

Snatch...hoo-ha...crotch...bush...cootch...beaver....V-J-Jay... cunt... pussy... goodies...pee ca choo...twat...cookoo...puss... cooter...clam...kitty...hen house...and the list goes on. Someday, let me know your word of choice so I can add it to the list.

Whatever name you choose is fine with me. But I do find that women need to swear while getting waxed. "Fuck" is hands down the number-one swear word in my wax rooms. There have been countless women who apologize like crazy because of the obscenities that come flying out of their mouths. Trust me; there is no need to apologize. Swearing doesn't faze me at all anymore.

After I finished doing a girl's Brazilian, I was waxing her eyebrows when she told me she was going home and hoped her boyfriend had left for work. When I asked her why, she said that he was psyched she had an appointment with me because it had been several months since she had gotten a wax. She knew not only would he want to see it, he'd want to touch it. Then she would have to explain to him that for a few hours she had a very "angry kitty" that wasn't ready to be touched and he'd have to wait. Men need to beware of the angry kitty.

Women also have all sorts of names for their clitoris, although the list isn't as fun. Many women refer to it as their "bean," which is a pretty accurate description in my opinion. Although I have instructed my children to always refer to their genitalia by their proper names, it can be hysterically funny to hear a woman scream obscenities at me as she abruptly sits up to make sure I didn't wax off her precious rose bud. When a woman is nervous and anxious about getting waxed, it is often hard to convince her that no matter how hard I pull, it would be impossible for me to remove her clit. But you'd be surprised how many women worry about it.

A girl came in one day pretty high on pot. Between the smell and red eyes, it didn't take a rocket scientist to figure out she had gotten high before she came in to see me. Maybe she thought it would give her courage to go through with the wax or simply make the service easier to deal with. She wasn't the first woman to come in stoned. People will do whatever is necessary to help them deal with an awkward and potentially painful experience. Her boyfriend came into the room with her as well, which is fairly common at our salon. Sometimes it makes the client more comfortable to have a friend or loved one in the room for support. She told me that she had a nightmare that I had waxed her clit off. Even though I told her repeatedly that it was impossible to remove it with hot wax, she was so nervous that she just couldn't lie still. In fact, she was so fidgety that it was extremely hard to wax her. Every time I pulled off a strip, she would sit up to check that her parts were still there. While she was cleaning up, she was still freaking out that I could have removed her fragile bud. She kept saying that her life would be ruined if she couldn't cum anymore. I even explained to her that the clitoris doesn't have hair on in so it didn't make sense to worry about it. That didn't seem to matter and reasoning with her wasn't even remotely possible. Guess the whole experience was too traumatizing for her, because she didn't come back.

I have to admit it seems pretty ridiculous that any remotely intelligent woman would think that a dollop of hot wax could remove the clitoris or any other body part, for that matter. Just for the record, body parts don't just appear on the strip after I have waxed them. It is impossible for me to remove your upper lip, kneecap, or clitoris.

I waxed a woman in her forties who was also obsessed with the idea of me ripping off her clit. Although it was obvious she was a little nervous getting her first wax, she was able to maintain a pretty good conversation for the first few minutes. All of a sudden she sat up and yelled, "Oh, my god, did you rip my clit off?" I assured her that I only removed her labia hair on the left side of her vagina and her clit remained intact. You see, I am normally able to remove the hair on one side of the vagina in one quick swipe. I admit it can be quite exhilarating (I love that adjective) and I think that sometimes clients feel like I have removed more than I intended. Ladies, feel confident that it would take more than some hot wax to remove your treasured pearl.

I have had hundreds of women convinced that their external genitalia are gushing blood because the pain is so intense. Although some women will experience a small amount of bleeding, no one has ever hemorrhaged at our salon.

The female anatomy is a unique, complicated thing. You never know what size, shape, or condition it will be in. The best you can do is expect nothing, be ready for the worst-case scenario, and be psyched when clean, thin hair is presented in your face. The honest truth is you never know what the pussy will be like until it is on the table, totally naked, in your face, and ready to be ripped.

Not only are there a lot of fun names for the pussy, people have fun names for me. A girl asked me how I ever decided to be a "pussy ripper" for a living. I can't really say for sure, except that I can't imagine doing anything else.

Once you say the word "pussy" a few times, you will find it comes out of your mouth pretty comfortably. I admit that, at first, it was awkward. But I totally got over it. A seventeen-year-old college freshman came in for a Brazilian. She asked if would be possible to get a letter left in place of where a landing strip would be. I said absolutely. She asked for the letter "P." So, being a smart ass, I said, "Oh, P for pussy?" Her face turned scarlet and she quietly said, "No, Patrick."

I have done letters in the past, but, honestly, they are a pain in the ass. When two girls came in together wanting letters, I was willing to do it. I just said it would be an additional five dollars because it takes more time. They were fine with the extra cost and were psyched to have their guys' initials down there. My response to each of them was I hoped they were easy letters like a "T" or an "L." The one girl said, "Oh, yeah, it's an easy letter. His name is Steven." Are you fucking kidding me! Soft blond pubic hair perfectly sculpted to the letter "S." So I asked her what her friend's man's name was, hoping it was easier. It was Kenneth. Shoot me.

When a woman reluctantly climbs on the table and tells me she had been to our salon three months ago and wouldn't let my girl wax the whole thing, I advised her sternly and decisively that no one gets off my table until she is bald. When your puss is in my face, I am in control. There's no turning back. I always finish.

Although the vagina seems like a mysterious entity, it really isn't. In my opinion, it is some randomly shaped folds of skin with some nasty hair on it. I like to tell women that their vagina reminds me of an elbow. It is simply a body part with creases in it.

So call your puss whatever you want. Scream any obscenity in any language that makes you feel better. Feel free to grab my wrist or arm if you need something to hang on to. In fact, I had a woman squeeze my ass through the entire service. When she realized what she was doing, she apologized. I told her since I was holding her vagina, it was okay for her to hold my ass. Bite on a towel. Chomp on a lollipop. Squeeze a friend's hand. Do your Lamaze breathing. Call me names. Ignore my questions. Put your hand over an area that I am about to wax and stick to your own skin. Close your legs and glue yourself shut. Kick me in the head. Curl your toes until they cramp. Do whatever you have to. I'll still finish. As I tell every uncooperative, resistant client: I always win.

What's That Smell?

When I asked Mark to read my book, he was completely disgusted by this chapter. He didn't understand why I put so much emphasis on hygiene. I'll tell you. I see a lot of dirty people every day and I hope this heightens awareness. In addition, when I blog about gross shit, people comment and like my posts more then any funny story. So, you are hereby forewarned that this chapter is descriptive and unpleasant with a few amusing antidotes thrown in.

Okay, folks, let's talk hygiene. This is probably the most important chapter in this book and I beg each and every one of you to pay really close attention to what I have to say. It seems like an obvious thing. You go for a procedure that requires removing your undergarments, and you prepare by doing what? The most obvious prerequisite in my mind is a thorough shower. Obvious? You'd think. Realistic? Not by a long shot. It is un-fucking-believable how unclean the average woman is.

So let's get down to the nitty-gritty on getting your lady parts prepared for a Brazilian wax. For starters, please take a shower fairly close to the time of your appointment. Within a few hours would be nice. Right before the appointment is ideal, but often not realistic. Although it seems like an obvious expectation, there are women who come in who haven't even showered the same day as the service. You think I am kidding? Think again.

Now, we need to discuss specifics. It is not a matter of fancy science but after all the nasty shit I have encountered, it definitely requires some in-depth discussion. Women have lots of folds and creases, so it is imperative that each fold be separated and washed as thoroughly as a surgeon who is entering an operating room. This is no longer a recommendation but a desperate plea. I don't understand why women don't scrutinize their body and make sure they are scrubbed thoroughly so there is never any odor or anything funky down there. It is a crazy thing for me to fantasize about, wouldn't you say? There is a lot of what I will call "debris" that gets collected in the folds of seemingly clean women. Even women with wet hair who have come to the salon directly from the shower will still have white or yellow residue in their creases. It's so gross. And it can really smell funky. I have a male friend who told me that after he read this part of the book, he could better understand why some of his friends don't like to go down on their women. I have understood that for years. In fact, if I have ever had any lesbian tendencies in the past, they have totally been obliterated. I have even come across vaginal discharge that has hardened and is all clumpy around the opening of the vagina. That crusty shit is enough to send me right over the edge. How the hell do you not see it, aside from the smell that accompanies it?

It would also be greatly appreciated if you cleaned the inside as well. The different colored and textured gunk that can collect inside a vagina does not resemble creative works of art. Most women tend to have fluids that live inside of them, which, at certain times, can be a wonderful thing. Before a wax, however, those fluids are not welcome. Cleaning out the entranceway is a form of common courtesy. You clean the inside of your toilet? Then clean the inside of your genitalia as well. It isn't difficult to clean out the opening. If you can't figure it out in the shower, a garden hose will do the trick.

I recently tweeted that there was a reason I don't eat yogurt. One of my clients responded by saying, "no you didn't." And my reply was "oh yes, I did."

In case you were wondering, I can tell if you have had sex that day. If there is no visible discharge, there is often a strong semen smell that can be quite overpowering. Often I can tell if you have had sex the night before by the lingering odor. So listen up: I don't want to be able to tell that you have recently had sex by a smell or by looking at the discharge seeping out. Over the years, I feel like I have acquired a PhD in discerning what went on between your legs. Be sneakier and disguise your lovemaking better. I don't want to see it or smell it. Over the years, I have started to refer to seminal fluids as a man's baby butter. It seems to be a nicer way of referring to his discharge. And, by the way, if your guy has a nasty funk to his fluid, tell him to eat more fruit.

I guess I can understand that every woman feels differently about her body. Many people are brought up to believe that the naked body is a very private thing or even a very vulgar thing. Some of us have been taught that we should feel ashamed about exploring our own body. If you aren't comfortable touching your own body to thoroughly clean it, then I guess I will try to be more understanding. But I implore you to try to be more open-minded about your anatomy. It's not as scary as you think.

I waxed a woman for more than ten years who had a rule that there was no sex for twenty-four hours prior to a wax. It was her way of being considerate to me. For a while, this woman, her best friend, and her sister made appointments together so they could all get waxed at the same time. They would all come into the room together and, as you can imagine, we had a lot of laughs. In fact, once they became comfortable with me and the salon, they started bringing beer with them. We had kind of a waxing party every four to six weeks. It was a lot of fun. Anyway, they all shared the no-sex rule, which I truly appreciated. Every once in a while they would bring additional friends in to get waxed with them and join in the festivities. They were always very conscientious about letting their friends know the rules they followed when it was time for wax day. None of them had sex for twenty-fours after, either, in case their body was sensitive. They wanted to avoid any more pain down there. That isn't always necessary, but sometimes it is a good idea to wait a few hours. Not only were these women a great part of my experience as a wax technician, their no-sex rule is one that any person getting waxed should follow.

Ladies, I hate to make you feel bad but one of my cleanest clients is a guy. As a rule, I do not do Brazilians on men. Too many of the requests for Brazilians we have gotten from men have been from perverts. They make sick innuendos on the phone and I can't be bothered, so I made the decision years ago to protect myself from being in an unsafe or uncomfortable position in a private room alone with a man by just declining to perform the service on guys altogether. Besides, men have really dense hair and it can be a real bitch to pull out. And, more importantly, the scrotum is a thin, delicate area that can easily tear. No thanks. I'll stick to women. Anyways, one of my regular female clients brought in her best friend, who just happens to be a guy. He wanted the crack in his ass waxed. It was awkward at first, but he was such a cool guy and was so incredibly clean that it ended up being a no-brainer and I continued to do him for several years. He found out that I had told his friend that he had a cleaner backside than most of my female clients. I think that made him feel kind of proud; at least I hope it did. He made quite a favorable impression on me. Want to make me happy? Power-wash your ass.

I have a woman that comes to the salon who sounds exactly like a dude on the phone. Every time she calls for a wax, I hesitate making the appointment. Fortunately she understands that her deep, raspy voice can be confused as a man's. She has learned now that she has to say who she is when she calls so we don't refuse to make an appointment for her.

Another hygiene issue that needs to be addressed is yeast infections. I have had several uncomfortable experiences with women who have come into the salon with an active yeast infection. For the record, if you wax over an area with a yeast infection, not only will it hurt a thousand times more than normal, your skin will be left red, raw, and miserable. And then it will take quite a while to heal, possibly until the hair starts growing back. Believe me, trying to rid the hair during this time isn't worth it. Besides, the odor and discharge that accompany a yeast infection is not something any technician wants to get face to face with. It often takes two months for the skin to thoroughly heal once the infection is gone and healing depends on how long the infection had gone untreated or just how bad the infection was. I have two incidents that remain vivid in my mind where a yeast infection has gotten in the way of the service.

I had been waxing a young girl for a year or two and during one of her visits I noticed a thick, smelly discharge at the entrance of her vagina. I asked her if she had a yeast infection and she adamantly denied having one. In fact, she said not only had she never had one, she didn't even really know what one was. I don't know how anyone cannot notice the itch, smell, or discharge that results from an infection. I concede that not everyone knows his or her body well, but come on! It is annoying, gross, and potentially contagious. And I am not going there. So after a quick lesson on how antibiotics can cause a secondary infection in our body, I told her that I wouldn't be able to wax her. I know she was embarrassed and I tried to be as informative and delicate with my discovery as possible, but I wouldn't jeopardize hurting her skin and I really didn't want to get that close to it. So I told her she needed to wait at least another month before we could even think about doing it.

I told this story to one of my clients. She couldn't believe that the girl didn't know she had a yeast infection. I mean, c'mon, they like to make their presence known in more ways than one. In her opinion, the girl probably didn't know her body well and was hoping that if she just pretended it wasn't there, it would just go away. Then this client had an interesting observation about how it feels to have an infection. She said, "How can you not know you have an infection when all you want to do is sit on a cork screw?" I had another client tell me she wanted to rub her bare bottom on her wool rug because the itch was driving her crazy.

The second incident was a woman my age (I'm in my forties) who was adamant that her infection was gone. I tried to be as diplomatic as possible, but the discussion wasn't going well. I noticed the cottage-cheese-like discharge pouring out of her and told her what I saw before I even touched her. She was insistent that the infection was gone and was getting pissed off that I even had the audacity to say something. I knew that if I waxed her lips, she would have been in a lot of pain and her puss would have been left as red as a third-degree sunburn. She had sensitive skin in a normal state, so I absolutely refused to risk hurting her even more. I got so frustrated that she wouldn't just concede that it was possible that it hadn't totally cleared. So I handed her a mirror and told her to check for herself and see the chunky white substance between her legs. Then she got kind of nervous because I think she was really hoping that it had cleared up so she could get a wax. I also think she was praying that I wouldn't notice. Believe me, I notice everything. Unfortunately, it became really uncomfortable in the room. She said her husband really wanted her waxed because they had something special planned that weekend. It sounded like he was a pretty controlling man and she seemed scared to go home without being bald. I didn't care. It hurts like hell to have sex when it's infected down there anyway. He'd have to suck it up and wait. Okay, maybe he wouldn't want to suck on it.

People often wonder if I have ever come across a genital disease. You would think that if someone had anything suspicious between their legs, they wouldn't come in to see me. But that isn't the case. One girl had a pretty serious case of genital warts. If you wax over warts, they can bleed and I feared they would spread. I didn't notice them right away. They were, however, fairly widespread on her underside. It sounded like her doctor was pretty cavalier in treating them. I advised her to be more aggressive in having them removed. I didn't want to aggravate them or encourage them to spread more rapidly, so she stopped getting waxed.

It is not worth it to wax someone if you know you are going to hurt her. Although we pay a lot for liability insurance, I pray we never need it. There is a lot of bad shit that can happen when you wax someone so you really need to pay attention to what you are doing. Bruising and bleeding can happen, so it is important to try to minimize the amount of trauma you cause to a woman's most intimate parts. I have removed several moles by accident that were hiding in dense pubic forests. I have also irritated countless skin tabs that grow randomly around the pubic and rectal area. Those suckers often get in the way and totally piss me off. I am not a doctor and I prefer not to remove excess skin growths, but it is often hard for me to tell when a person has a small mole hiding under a massive 1970s bush garden. What really sucks about waxing over growths is that the pubic area is so vascular that any irritation to a mole or skin tab can cause a ton of bleeding. Band-Aids or mini-pads are a must-have in the wax room, even if they are rarely used.

We had a girl come in with visible tears around her rectum. My employee was hesitant to wax that area because the skin was so irritated and unhealthy. We never want to wax over an area that is cut or chafed. What she didn't have the nerve to ask was why the client had all the cuts back there. I have no problem asking questions. It is my honest narrative with my clients that has made it possible for me to share such great stories with everyone. From the description of the area, it sounded like the client had anal sex that was very traumatizing to her skin. From spending so much time looking at rectums, I have noticed that anal sex has become very popular. One of my regulars even told me that she read that "anal is the new oral."

One time I waxed over a skin tab on a client and half of it pulled away from the skin. She hated the little growth and had complained about it as long as I had known her. Most women just live with the growths and don't go to a doctor to have them removed. Personally, they drive me crazy and whenever one surfaces, I have it cut off. Anyway, she asked for a towel to sit on, a hand mirror, tweezers, and scissors. She proceeded to sit on the floor in front of a window that allowed for more light, and cut the rest of it off.

Speaking of growths, I had a graduate student come in for a thigh and Brazilian wax. When her leg was straight up in the air, I noticed a bump the size of a golf ball in the crease of her buttocks. I don't think that most people generally feel that part of their body, where the top of the thigh and the butt meet, and I wouldn't have noticed it if her leg was down. I asked her what the bump was and she had no idea. I gave her a mirror so she could look at it and I had her feel it as well. She never noticed that there was a bump under her skin. She went to the doctor that week and they removed it right away thinking that it could be something serious. Happy to say it was a benign tumor and, once removed, she was fine. She said it was a little strange for her to explain to the doctor how it was discovered, but she was grateful for my discovery and the fact that I was forward enough to point it out to her. Whether you see a growth, a rash, or some nasty discharge, be honest with your client. If she ended up having lymphoma and I didn't say anything, I would have felt like shit.

Another hygiene issue that sometimes interferes with the waxing service is hemorrhoids. I understand that the current population tends to be overweight and I am okay with that, but why do we have to be constipated as well? I mean, isn't that why we often get those annoying, bulbous growths that protrude from our rectum? I know that our crappy American diets have a lot to do with our lousy bowel movements, but let me tell you something: hemorrhoids are gross. I have seen all sizes, shapes, and colors. Sometimes there is only one, but often there are clusters. There are times when they become inflamed and swollen and I have to be very careful to stay far away from them. In any case, they require extra care in keeping clean. I don't know the best way to advise cleaning your ass when it has hemorrhoids; I'm just telling you to do a better job. Some of my clients do a great job of cleaning around them and I could care less that they have them, but, more often than not, that's not the case. One of my clients went to four different doctors before she found one who would surgically remove them. One of the doctors had the nerve to say that they shouldn't matter at her age. She was forty. Hello… they are disgusting. Getting rid of them is a great idea. Ask a lady who looks closely at a lot of assholes every day.

Now it's time to get back to the thorough cleansing discussion that should occur prior to a wax. So let's discuss the hygiene that is required when cleaning your rectal area. More concentrated scrutiny must be taken in cleaning this area. It is beyond disgusting when you rip the hair off someone's rectum and there is brown debris all over the strip. Don't people know how to clean their ass? I have never discussed it with a client because I would hate to embarrass anyone and, when it happens, I don't discuss it with my husband or employees. I just get a new stick, finish the area, and move on. But, a few months ago, my new employee was completely grossed out when she had that happen to her. She was absolutely flabbergasted. She couldn't understand how someone could come in for a wax unless they had thoroughly cleaned the entire area. If you take a shower then have a bowel movement, please find a way to rewash your backside. I have seen so much brown residue on my strips that it is a wonder I haven't thrown in the towel on this Brazilian business years ago. Some people just don't give a shit and definitely don't know how to clean up after they've taken one.

A woman came in recently whom I hadn't seen in years. I love it when clients return after a prolonged absence. I understand that they can't always afford to continue coming and I am just psyched when they decide to come back. I love getting caught up on what has gone on in their lives during their time away from me. Anyway, this woman hadn't dated in over a year and decided it was time to get back into dating mode again. That is when a lot of women come to see me. It is a way of getting their body groomed and ready for action again. And coming to see me is often part of the preparation, especially since being bald is the new craze. Since her hair was long and tended to hold a lot of moisture, her doctor had suggested she use baby powder between her legs. Unfortunately the mix of long hair, moisture, and baby powder can result in clumps of powder all around the vaginal opening. She wouldn't have used the powder if the doctor hadn't recommended it and she found it dried out her skin and made it very uncomfortable. I just found that the excessive use of baby powder resulted in a clumpy mix of discharge and powder, which was very unpleasant. For the record, using baby powder is not synonymous with good hygiene. Especially when it gets damp and globs. Get the picture. Ugh.

So who was the nastiest person I have ever waxed? Although I have had many award-winning cases over the years, there are a couple that really stand out. When Brazilians first started becoming popular, I was determined to wax any person that walked into the salon. In fact, I had a very large bikini wax clientele at the time and was encouraging everyone to try it. There are times that I probably should have been more discriminating, but I was determined to wax as many as possible because I knew that was the only way for me to master this absurd service that I suddenly found was becoming my "new normal". We usually close at three o'clock on Saturdays but I stayed late one Saturday for a girl who really wanted a wax. I remember that it was a beautiful day out, so I waited for her on our front porch. My in-laws converted an old farmhouse into the salon, which my husband and I now own, and we have a beautiful, large porch that wraps around the front of the house.

I was waiting for this college student who had been to the salon before, so she wasn't a stranger to me. When she showed up, I knew something was up. She looked like hell. I quickly found out that she had gone out the night before and was still pretty hung over. But I had waited so long for her; we went upstairs so I could get the wax over with. Try to picture this. She had her period. It was evident because it was everywhere. She had spent the afternoon cleaning her apartment barefoot and her feet were black. She never showered after her night out or at all on Saturday because she was determined to get her apartment cleaned—not sure what the correlation is between the two. She smelled like booze. She had dried blood all over her private area. Her body odor was pungent because it was summertime and she was sweaty. And to top it off, even her backside was messy. So the girl comes into the salon, strips from the waist down, hops up onto my table to get waxed, and is filthy. What do you say? I was absolutely dumbfounded. I had waited an hour for this?

So I sucked it up, put on my gloves, and went through many popsicle sticks putting the wax on and many strips ripping it off. So think about it: how would you deal with this situation? If I wasn't descriptive enough, let me reiterate: she could not have been any dirtier. But I did it. Anything for a buck sometimes. Believe me, this wasn't worth it. So we now have baby wipes everywhere in the salon and we strongly encourage everyone to use them.

But, I ask you, once she was undressed on the table, what is the best way to delicately say that it would have been appreciated if she took a shower before she came into the salon? What I really wanted to say was, "Are you fucking kidding me!"

I had another girl who came in with extremely long pubic hair, more than an inch in length. Just because hair is long doesn't mean it has to be dirty or clustered with dried, clumpy discharge. But this particular woman with her extremely long pubic hair gets an Oscar for the absolutely worst-smelling snatch I have ever had the displeasure to meet. She met a man online who lived quite far from Rochester. She had only hooked up with him once before. Apparently he found her hair distasteful (like the pun?) and asked her to groom it before she came to see him again. Well, I can see why he asked her to do something with it. It smelled not only like something had died down there, but then someone decided to douse the area with a putrid kind of ammonia. I have never encountered such a foul odor in my entire life. The smell was so strong, I felt sick to my stomach the rest of the day. In fact, we couldn't use that particular wax room for several hours because the smell lingered in there.

I usually say to my clients as they are leaving the salon that I hope to see them again in a month, but I couldn't say that to her. Hopefully making her bald helped her out a little bit with the odor, but I imagine that she will need a lot more help than I was able to give her.

Usually when there is a putrid smell between your legs, there are two possible scenarios that come to mind. One is that you may need to take a shower and thoroughly wash between your folds. The other is that there could be some kind of infection down there and you should really have it checked out. In either instance, it isn't an appropriate time to get waxed.

Often there are outward signs that, if you pay attention, will alert you to a potential nasty vaginal encounter. When you come across someone who is pretty shaky and outwardly unclean, rest assured, the underneath ain't gonna be pretty. A nail client of mine always has a lot of debris under her nails, food in her teeth, and very greasy hair. We found out after years of her coming to the salon that she had a drug addiction. When she called to inquire about getting a Brazilian, she asked what preparation was needed before she came in. My employee at the time told her, in a very direct manner, that she needed to take a shower first. My husband got pissed at our employee because it came across as fairly rude. When she told him who was asking to get waxed, he fully understood. Sometimes being straight-forward in a diplomatic manner is the only way.

Let's move away from that body part for now to another important one: your feet. When you lift your leg in the air, your foot is in my face. Believe it or not, foot odor can knock you out. Years ago, this girl used to bring this foot spray into the salon and spray her feet right before she would climb up on the table. It always seemed like a silly ritual, but, since then, I have fantasized about certain clients spraying their piggies as well. Some people come straight from the shower and their feet still smell rancid. Some women are aware of their foot odor and will keep their shoes on even if it makes them feel silly since they have no pants on. There are even more that I don't think even realize how bad the problem is. Or maybe they hope I won't notice. Trust me, I notice. I have thought about buying foot spray for the really foul-smelling ones, but, once again, that is a difficult subject to bring up once a lady is bare-assed in front of you. I'd hate to insult anyone or hurt her feelings, but sometimes I feel like I am going to be sick. I never knew feet could smell so bad.

Aside from hairspray, I'm not a huge fan of things that spray out of a can. The foot spray was actually in a pump form so the client wasn't using an aerosol in the room. I must admit that I have actually entertained the thought several times over the years that bug spray could come in handy. Especially when one of my nurses referred to a case of crabs that she encountered at the hospital as "crotch crickets."

Another hygiene issue is your breath. It may not seem important to you, but it is for me. Whenever I eat something at work, I brush my teeth. If I have had something with onions or garlic, not only do I brush my teeth, I suck on a breath mint. It seems like a considerate thing to do when you are face to face with a client. Okay, folks, oral hygiene would be appreciated from you as well. Sometimes it is extremely difficult to wax your face when there is food in your teeth or your breath is really bad. Just think of it this way: if you want perfectly groomed eyebrows, come with good oral hygiene so I don't have to rush. Feel free to peek up your nose as well. Hate seeing stuff hanging out of your nose. Boogers tend to really gross me out. Doesn't take long to peek in your rearview mirror before you enter the salon and stick a piece of gum in your mouth. Just a suggestion.

Back to the puss…at the end of your period, there is often a discolored residue, which can be very unpleasant. It can be brown, dried blood perhaps or a funky-colored discharge. I had a college student with a collection of dark brown residue at the entrance of her vagina. It was messy and smelled. It was very awkward but more often than not I seem to be put in these kinds of situations. Her girlfriend was in the room with her and saw all the brown crap all over the strip when I ripped it off. She thought I had made her bleed. I said that the color was just from her skin. I tried to be evasive because I didn't want to embarrass the girl. Thank God I wear gloves, have a strong stomach, and buy popsicle sticks in mass quantities. The thick yellow substance that can ooze at the end of your period can have quite a pungent smell. If your cycle isn't totally, one hundred percent over, please take a thorough shower then put a clean tampon in before you come into the room.

Can you get waxed when you have your period? If your flow can be contained with a fresh, clean tampon then I have absolutely no problem with it. You definitely may be more sensitive and some people are more prone to bruising during that time, but sometimes that is the only time that will work with your schedule. When a thirty-something called and said she had an appointment with me but had just gotten her period, my husband told her to put a new tampon in when she got to the shop. When she came into the room a few hours later, she asked me if I knew that she had called and spoken to Mark. I didn't know because we had been too busy for him to mention it to me but when she explained why she called, I said basically the same thing my husband said. I told her that as long as she had a fresh tampon in, I was fine. That was when she advised me that she didn't wear tampons. When I told Mark later, he was just infuriated. What are these people thinking?

So my plea to anyone thinking about pursuing that perfectly primped pussy: prepare better. Do a better job of washing every bit of your body inside and out. Do a better job of pulling your lips apart and cleaning inside your creases. Do a better job of washing your ass. Think of it this way: prepare yourself like you would for a date with a gorgeous guy who has told you all he wants to do is go down on you.

Guys Are the Real Pussies

Hot wax on the most intimate parts may make a woman nervous, but I have yet, in over fifteen years, had a woman pass out on the table or anywhere in the room, for that matter. Men, on the other hand, are a whole different story. There is a reason why women have been chosen to re-populate the world; guys cannot handle pain!

As I mentioned before, I made the decision years ago not to perform Brazilians on men, although I have made a few exceptions. Often they say inappropriate things on the phone when they call and I'd rather not be stuck face to penis in a private room with some pervert. And I really don't think it would be smart to risk my personal safety by going into a room on the second floor of our salon with some man I don't know and having him drop his drawers. There was an incident with a man from a town an hour from Rochester who was going from salon to salon getting his entire pubic area waxed. When he was left to clean up and get dressed, he would ejaculate all over the table. He called our salon, but we refused to do him. We even had the sheriff's department call us looking for any information about this guy so they could find him and have him arrested. On the phone, he mentioned the town he was from, which is what gave his identity away. Rumor has it that they did find him and he was arrested.

Several years ago I had a guy call me for a full body wax. He seemed legitimate on the phone and it sounded like a fun challenge for me to wax someone's entire body. To be safe, I decided to try to figure out if the call was legitimate or not, so I asked him how big he was. If he said ten inches, I would have refused him, but he said six feet, one hundred sixty pounds. It sounded like it was an honest request. Fortunately he wasn't that tall or heavy of a guy. I started on his upper body, which went pretty well. As I started working on his legs, he started to quiver. Shaking is fairly common when you cause pain to someone so I understood why his body was responding this way. I also have had women get the shakes when I am working on their bikini area, even though it isn't a long service. As I got to the private parts of his body, he was shaking so violently that he had to physically hold his jaw together because his teeth were chattering so badly. He actually used both hands to hold his mouth closed. It was unreal. I offered not to finish but he was determined to have me wax his entire body. His shaking got so violent that I thought he was going to pass out. I finished his body in sixty-five minutes. I still can't believe how quickly I was able to complete the service considering how miserable he was and how poorly his body was reacting. He was still shaking uncontrollably when he left the salon. He returned a few months later to do it again.

When he came the second time, he complained that I wasn't thorough enough in the genital area. In my defense, I told him that it was really difficult to get a clean wax with his intense body shaking. He said it took several hours for the shaking to subside. I was thankful that his body didn't have any external problems, such as a rash, acne breakout, or bruising. The second time went better. I was able to be more thorough and it didn't take quite as long since his hair wasn't quite as dense. He still shook, but not as badly.

Often men will continuously move to create a distraction from what I am doing. One of our friends wanted his back waxed.

Throughout the entire service, he kicked his feet constantly. It looked like he was swimming.

Several of my guys pull away from me every time I pull off a strip. If it's hard for you to keep still, don't worry: you are definitely not alone.

I once had a guy come in for a back wax who had a special request. He also wanted his nipples waxed. I had waxed his back before and that had always gone well. His chest had no hair on it but his nipples did have long, stringy hair on them. It took one swipe per nipple to remove the hair. When he went to sit up, his eyes rolled back and he fell back onto the pillow and started to shake and sweat. He could not stand the pain of having his nipples waxed, and the reaction he had to it was much more intense than I could have ever anticipated. I wax women's nipples all the time and they never even complain that it hurts. We had to hang out for a while until he felt calm enough to get up. I thought about getting him water or some hard candy but I didn't want to leave him unattended and risk him falling off the table. When he finally was ready to get up, I helped him dress. When we went down to the waiting room, I helped him sign his credit card because he was shaking too badly to sign it himself. As he was leaving, I apologized for the way he responded to the wax, because I never saw it coming. He was supposed to go see his girlfriend at work after he left the salon but he decided to go home and rest instead. He assured me that he would be able to drive himself.

After he left, my husband and the man he was working on were worried about what I had done to this guy that caused me to apologize. They expected something way more interesting than a nipple wax, but nipples were the truth. We now have smelling salts and intercoms in each wax room.

I had my first person pass out completely into an unconscious state in 2008. And, yes, it was a man. It was a Saturday morning and one of my girls brought her boyfriend in to get his back done. Normally, after I finish waxing a man's back, I sit the guy up to do his shoulders. When he got off the table to get dressed, he stumbled across the room, hit his head on a closet door, and collapsed between a chair and a coat rack. When he was stumbling, his girl and I thought he was busting our chops and we just watched him as he fell. He was only knocked out for a few minutes but he was dazed and confused for several minutes after that. When he came to, we noticed he got scraped up from falling against the wooden door. We were more worried because he began to sweat so profusely. A cold compress, a vitamin C drink, and sitting next to an open window to have the cold breeze blow on him helped him recover.

One of the comical parts of this scenario is while he was sitting in a chair trying to regain his composure, his girl asked me if I was still willing to wax her. You see, she was scheduled to get a Brazilian that morning after I finished his back. So while he was sipping on his drink, I gave his girl a wax. It seemed a little strange since he was sitting there so out of sorts, but I had the time. As it turned out, he was a sports coach and always wondered what it felt like to pass out since he had many players in his career get knocked unconscious. Now he knew. I was glad I could help out. I tracked him down on the following Monday to see how he was doing. He had no idea what my name was so he was confused as to who was calling. Once he figured it out, he said he had a stiff neck (probably whiplash) but otherwise was okay. Next time I saw her, they had broken up.

Generally I don't like to do men is because their scrotum is so thin and so sensitive. One of my guys has a scar from where some skin came off the area right next to his testicles. It was pretty creepy. Have you ever shaved your legs and took a hunk of skin off? Your skin turns white and it won't stop bleeding? Yeah, that's what happened. Not fun. He still comes back to me and I still wax that area on him, but I felt so awful about leaving a permanent mark on him. I guess the price of beauty doesn't just refer to women.

There is a man in his forties who has been getting waxed by me for years who has admitted that he comes to me for the counseling as well as the hair removal. He is still single and has stories, issues, and questions that he likes to share with a woman his age who isn't a threat, doesn't pass judgment, and will listen and try to offer any advice possible. We have such a good rapport that I feel comfortable yelling at him when he's being selfish or narrow-minded about a relationship issue or when he is just being a guy. Getting rid of the hair on his torso actually helps control his acne, but I really believe he comes to me to talk more than anything else. He is a really nice guy, and I enjoy our time together. When he had one of my employees wax him, he told me she did fine but he missed the conversation with me. She was too young and pretty for him to have the same kind of open and honest discussion. He did figure out one of my strategies, however. I tend to ask my clients a question and as they are about to answer, I rip a strip off. I try to perform the service using this technique because it can be an excellent distraction from the pain I will be inflicting upon them. I was working on his chest and he was hesitating to answer me so I was teasing him that he needed to answer. All of a sudden he said, "Is this some kind of psychology or something?" Yep, it sure is!

One day he called me and said he needed a wax and that it was kind of an emergency. When he took off his shirt, I noticed several hickeys on his neck. His girlfriend was planning on moving into his house so he had one last fling with this young, hot girl that he liked screwing. He didn't want the girlfriend to notice the hickey's so he figured if he got a wax, he could blame me for the marks on his neck.

As I mentioned earlier, one of my regular female clients brought a friend in to have the crack in his ass waxed. Attention, gentlemen: not a bad idea. You guys can really grow some hair back there. I was apprehensive at first because male rectal hair can be really difficult to extract, but it worked well. In fact, he was very clean and well-groomed and now I actually wax other intimate parts of him as well. We did have one bad experience together but it had nothing to do with his private areas. One time when he came in and went to sit down on the table (now remember, he was bare-assed), my massage table collapsed under him. I wax a lot of obese people these days. The legs of the table were made out of wood and they must have been stressed. Two of the opposing legs collapsed underneath him. They actually shattered into hundreds of pieces. It was like a crude comedy sketch. Fortunately, his reactions were quick and he jumped off the table so quickly that he didn't fall to the ground. I was so glad that he wasn't hurt. Embarrassed, yes, but not hurt. He was really cool about it and still comes in. We now have massage tables with metal legs.

My massage tables have approximately a three-hundred-pound weight limit. This has never been an issue with my guys, but, unfortunately, it is becoming a huge issue with some of my girls. A three-hundred-and-forty-pound woman came in for a Brazilian and my table, which has never made any creaking sounds, was singing in pain. I don't mind waxing bigger people. I just needed to buy industrial-strength tables.

Not everybody realizes that the name of our salon refers to my husband, Mark, and me, Mary Elizabeth. That's where the salon name of "Mark & M.E." originated. When a new, male client comes into the salon and acts all flirty, I always bring into the conversation that Mark is downstairs and that he is my husband. The men looking for a prospective date often switch to one of my single employees the next time they come in. I love the name of the salon. I think it's catchy. One of my clients' husbands asked her when she was going back to Mike and Chuck's, because he really loved her Brazilian wax. At first, she wasn't sure what he was talking about. He never paid that much attention to the name of the salon. He knew it was two names and he knew he wanted her to make another appointment with me. He just got the names a little mixed up. I guess I am Chuck.

I had a newly married couple come in recently. They had been married one month and were getting ready to go on their honeymoon. She has been coming to me for a few years and I had waxed his back twice before. We were having a discussion on grooming the male genitalia. It is a fairly common discussion that takes place in our salon. You see, if we women are willing to put hot wax on such a sensitive part of our body then rip the hair out from the root, we'd like to believe that our companions would go to some effort to keep their parts groomed as well. Apparently this couple had named the process that he went through to clean up his junk. This man wanted to share his grooming title with me but felt the need to get permission from his wife first. She told him that he could say anything in front of me so I found out that he makes sure his parts are "blow-job friendly." I just smiled. We girls appreciate their effort and I told him as much.

Another guy told me that the only benefit to having a girlfriend living out of town was that he didn't have to groom as often. He thought shaving was a pain and he hated how bad it itched when it grew back.

Okay, gentlemen, if you are going to shave, we have some rules. You must keep it up on a regular basis. And we are referring not only to your genitalia, but your face as well. We do not appreciate a five o'clock shadow on your face or between our legs. Thank you.

47

We had a frat boy from a local college lose a bet. The guys had a bet that if he didn't lose twenty-five pounds by spring break then he would have to get some body part waxed. And the brothers would decide what part. Four guys brought him in for a chest wax. Man, was he hairy. They filmed the experience. Remember the movie *The Forty-Year-Old Virgin?* They had us wax patterns in his chest while he screamed like a baby. The footage of his face really belonged on YouTube because he looked like he was being tortured. As he was leaving the salon, he was actually walking funny, which didn't make sense since we didn't wax below the belt. He said he would never step foot in our salon again. And he never did.

When a foreign male student walked in without an appointment for an underarm wax, I was happy to be of service. We have students from all over the world who come to the salon and that makes our experiences with our clients even more interesting. He did pretty well with the underarms. Then asked me if I did the backside. He had a strong accent and was definitely difficult to understand so I pointed to my buttocks to confirm his request. He actually meant the crack in his ass. "Sure, I do that." So we went upstairs and he said he really wanted the front done. I told him that I wouldn't do that but I'd be happy to wax his backside. He yelled like a baby as I waxed his crack and that definitely confirmed to him why he wouldn't want the front side waxed. He never would have been able to handle it. For men, waxing their genitalia sounds like a great idea until I actually get near that area with hot wax. It is no joke. Their boys are sensitive.

A man complained that his friends at the gym repeatedly ridiculed him because his back hair was so dense. They told him it looked like he had a sweater on his back. He came in reluctantly to get a back wax because that was what his best friend in New York City told him to do. I knew that the wax would be really painful because his hair was so long and dense. So I started my chatty conversation with him, and he started to sweat and to swear and to mumble and to moan. Then he asked me to hold on a second so he could get his phone. He called his best friend once he got back on the table and yelled and swore at him like he was going to beat the shit out of him next time they were together. I was happy he didn't take out his aggression on me because he was giving his friend a really hard time. When I finished, he told me that he would just wear a shirt that covered more of his body at the gym. He couldn't handle the wax and needed to learn how to ignore the mocking of his buddies.

Arms are actually a little tricky to wax because of the different directions the hair grows in. They also tend to be more awkward to get at every side. I have waxed several men's arms in my career and I have to say that I really like the look. When a man has muscular arms, the definition is so much better without hair in the way. And it happens to be one body part that really doesn't hurt very much.

One of my college guys gets his legs waxed. When we first met, I asked him why he wanted his legs done. Was he a swimmer perhaps? No. He just couldn't stand how his leg hair felt against his socks; the way his socks pulled at his lower leg hair drove him crazy. He had some OCD issues and his hair on his legs really bugged him. He tried shaving but he said not only was it a pain, it was too itchy and scratchy growing in. Men's legs are generally more muscular than women's, so they are pretty easy to wax. I do find, however, that women handle the pain much better during a leg wax even though we tend to be less firm. He wriggled around a bit, but, for the most part, handled it pretty well. Hopefully, he found a new wax technician he liked when he graduated and moved out of town. If he didn't, I imagine he doesn't wear socks anymore.

A med student came in for a leg wax and squirmed like crazy on the table. He was trying so hard to keep his composure but he had really thick, dark hair that was difficult to pull out, so I know it had to hurt like hell. When I finished up and oiled his legs to get some of the wax residue off, he stood in front of the mirror and did weightlifting poses. He was so excited to see his muscular definition in his legs. His body was incredibly defined, but it was really hard to notice with all of the hair covering it. I waxed him again the following month with his girlfriend in the room and, boy, was he more macho! It should have been less painful because he didn't have quite as much hair as he had the first time around, but he did a much better job of masking the pain the second time.

A couple months later I saw him walking through our neighborhood as I was driving to work and pulled over to ask him why he hadn't come in again. He got a little embarrassed and said he "just couldn't take it." In this business, that sentiment is one I have to accept.

One of my regular back clients asked me if he could ask for a special request. I got nervous because I hate saying no to anyone, but I really didn't want to give him a wax in his private area. He is six-five and weighs close to three hundred pounds. His back takes a fair amount of time and his hair grows really thick. So I hesitantly said, "What do you want?" He said, "Could you please wax my feet?" I started laughing hysterically. "Is that all?" He couldn't figure out why I was laughing so hard and why I looked so surprised. I told him I was afraid he wanted a bikini wax and would have felt bad saying no to him. He informed me that I would never be going there.

On another occasion, this same man came in for a back wax and, once again, had a special request. He is married with two kids and they were going on a family vacation. He told me that his wife would be calling for a bikini wax before they left. I have given her bikini waxes before, so I couldn't figure out what the request was at first. He wanted me to accidently give her a Brazilian instead of a bikini and he promised he would compensate me with a big tip. I couldn't stop laughing. I wasn't sure how I would pull this off. I told him that it would be difficult to wax her labia without her noticing. Should I just say, "Whoops"? Later that day, she called for an appointment and I had to try really hard not to laugh as I was writing her name in the book. When she came in, she removed her panties (which I have even my regular bikini clients do) and I asked her if she wanted a landing strip or triangle. We started talking, and I proceeded to give her a Brazilian.

A few hours later, I heard my husband say, "Are you looking for my wife?" I walked into the waiting room and the husband was standing there with a twenty-dollar bill in his hand. He told me that he needed to show me something. He took out his phone and showed me a text from his wife. It said, "Went in for a bikini, left with a Brazilian. Not sure how that happened. LOL." He gave me a big hug, thanked me, and went on his way.

The first back I ever waxed was probably one of the hardest jobs I have ever done. He was a chunky, shy graduate student. His hair was very long and dense and I had to trim it first. It was obviously very painful for him. Blood seeped through the pores after each rip. When I finished getting the stickiness off and treating the skin with a mild antiseptic, he stood up and put an undershirt on. Then he started to cry. He told me that he had never taken off his shirt at the beach or ever let any woman see him without a shirt on. Since he was a young teen, he had been mortified by his massive amount of body hair. He said that other students mocked him relentlessly. He couldn't believe the way his bare skin felt against his undershirt. He was so happy about having no hair on his body that once he stopped crying, he gave me a big hug and told me that he was forever indebted to me.

Men can be just as concerned with the way their bodies look as women are. Their hair can be a source of embarrassment and annoyance as well. Since the majority of my clients are women, it is a treat working on a man. It can be a great diversion from the string of vaginas that come through the salon each day. But, for the most part, men are a lot less tolerant of the whole hot wax and ripping experience. But that's okay. They can be so much fun to mock! Men definitely are the real pussies.

So What Kind of Woman Waxes It All?

Actually, I have found that every type of woman waxes. Every age, size, ethnicity...it is a trend that crosses all stereotypical boundaries. What has astounded me the most are all of the heavy women who wax. This is definitely an era where more people are overweight, and it thrills me that so many of these women are paying just as much attention to that area as the little skinny girls that pass through our salon. It doesn't matter to me at all what size a woman is as long as she is clean. With overweight people, the hair can cause even more rash and irritation because of the folds in the skin, so it can be a huge improvement to the condition of the skin in that area if the hair is removed. It can also be logistically difficult to shave that area for some of my more obese clients, so waxing is the perfect alternative. It's a lot easier for me to get to that area than it is for them, so bring it on.

I've had people ask me if it is harder to wax a bigger person, and I would be lying if I didn't admit that sometimes it can be quite difficult. But, for the most part, it really doesn't matter. I have several big girls who are so incredibly flexible that it would put a lot of thinner women to shame. I went in the room with a young woman who was about a hundred and fifty pounds overweight. She was really nervous about getting undressed in front of me and told me she even felt nervous taking her pants off. I told her that we all had the same parts and, as long as she was clean, I couldn't care less how big she was. After we talked for a few minutes and I assured her that it really didn't matter to me, she undressed and hopped on the table. When I asked her to lift her left leg up and hold it for me so I could wax down under, she actually set her leg onto the pillow next to her head. My immediate response was, "Wow, you are flexible for a big girl!" She started laughing, and I could tell that my honesty made her feel even more at ease. We chatted the whole time and developed an immediate rapport. As she was getting ready to leave the salon, she gave me a hug and thanked me for making what could have been a humiliating experience very comfortable and even fun. My response to her flexibility was honest and spontaneous. I really think people appreciate honesty.

So what about the woman who has lost a ton of weight and has lots of extra skin? We have several clients who have had fat-reduction surgeries, like gastric bypass or the lap-band. The dramatic weight loss often results in an abundance of extra skin. Not only is the stretched-out skin more difficult to keep taut, but it is often more difficult to keep clean. I have found that stretched skin tends to be more sensitive, and many of the women don't keep up with waxing because it is just too painful. Even when surgery is performed to fix the skin, the flattened skin that remains tends to be very fragile. So please be extra careful.

Any body is capable of being waxed. Believe it or not, the pussy on a big girl isn't really that much bigger than that of a skinny little thing. There are some logistical issues, however, that need to be taken into consideration when waxing an obese person. Unfortunately, I found out the hard way what happens when a three-hundred-pound woman rolls on her side to the edge of the table to have her rectum waxed without first readjusting her weight on the table. The table falls over. So, the moral of the story: have your client scoot to the left of the table before she rolls on her right. In hindsight, it seems like a pretty obvious assessment of the situation, but, at the time, it was mortifying to have the table fall over. So now I know that it is better to be safe then crumpled in a heap on the floor. The other lesson to be learned here is to buy an industrial-strength table. Not only are my tables sturdier now, they have a hydraulic option to make it easier for me to get to a woman's parts.

Not every woman is flexible and that can make the actual waxing procedure a little more complicated. Not every hip can turn out and not every leg can go straight up in the air. Every woman is unique. Flexibility cannot be determined by age or size. A woman can put her leg over her head or not. Is it easier when a woman is flexible? Without a doubt. Is it common? Not really. I encourage every woman to do a little yoga now and again. It makes my life way easier.

So what about pregnant women? Can they get a wax? Absolutely. I am convinced that the '70s video they show in Lamaze class is responsible for the influx of pregnant women seeking a bald passageway for their baby to exit. If you haven't been to a birthing class, then you haven't had the privilege of seeing a baby born out of a vagina that is so hairy that you cannot distinguish the difference between the top of the baby's head and the hair on the lips of the woman giving birth. One woman told me that while she was watching the video with her husband, she asked him if she looked like that down there. He said, "Yeah, kind of." She came to see me a few days later.

It is definitely more challenging to wax a woman who is noticeably pregnant. For starters, I have to be more careful not to compromise their low back, so I make sure these women don't place both legs straight in front of them. I make certain that one leg is bent at all times. There is also more blood and swelling in the genitalia, so I have to be more conscientious and be sure that I don't cause unnecessary bruising or bleeding in the area. The skin is so much more sensitive that I really need to pay extra attention to how the skin is responding to the whole waxing experience. And there will be certain times when the skin just doesn't respond well. So just don't do it. Give the client a simple bikini wax if possible and call it a day.

The only complication that has made it difficult for me to wax that area is when the woman develops engorged varicose veins in her labia. It looks like varicose veins that people have in their legs; it just happens in the genital area. It is very painful for the expectant mama and very dangerous for me to wax. I have encountered women with such severe cases that they have had to wear a female type of jock strap to hold the lips securely against the body. When engorged labia hang, the pain is excruciating. It is crucial that you never wax over an area with a vein or you could cause the woman to hemorrhage. Who would have thought a hair-removal service would have such liability?

So we know that it is more painful to wax while pregnant. Why do we do it? We wax while we are pregnant because we are heavier, sweatier, and more paranoid of moisture and odor while numerous, random people are hanging out between our legs. I delivered my children at a teaching hospital and it was pretty annoying to have random medical folk come in and check out what was happening between my legs. If one more resident stuck their hand up me to determine how dilated I was, I was going to start throwing punches. I have to say I was glad that I was groomed down there and I understand why other pregnant women are concerned with how they look. Being groomed makes us more confident as our parts are exposed to the world.

The labia come in all shapes and sizes, which makes each encounter unique. One of my girls has the biggest outer lips I have ever seen. They look like hot dog buns. I am not exaggerating. They look like the size, shape, and color of hot dog buns. In fact, she likes to boast about her big lips. She even told me that her man loves her lips so much that he likes to hold on to them and gently caress them when they are hanging out. Because they are so big, he just likes to rub them. He finds it very comforting. It is an interesting scenario to visualize, especially since I have met the guy. I like to imagine that he is a huge baseball fan and likes to cradle his hot dog buns while watching the game.

We have a lot of professional women who come into the salon. Often they find themselves in the midst of a business conversation on the phone when they come in for their appointment. Since I book every fifteen minutes, I don't always have time to wait for their phone call to end in order to give them a wax. So I will signal for them to undress while I get my gloves on. I have waxed countless women while they spoke to someone on the phone, whether it is a personal or business call. It does toughen them up since it they usually don't feel comfortable yelling about the pain or admitting what they were doing during the conversation.

One time a woman in her forties was talking to her boyfriend while she was getting her wax. He had a ton of questions about the position of her body, what I was exactly doing, and even about what I looked like. I would rather not imagine what he was doing on the other end of the phone call. He kept asking how many strips I had left to pull. I don't count so I was no help in that regard. He found the whole process intriguing and told her that next time she should videotape the service so he could watch it over and over again. I found that a little creepy.

Women often want a wax before they get married. We call it the "honeymoon Brazilian wax." Unfortunately, women like to be tan for their wedding as well. Back in the '80s, we were prone to hang out in tanning beds to achieve that beautifully bronzed Florida look. Now it is much more socially acceptable to get a spray tan. Attention, ladies: if you get a spray tan before a wax, I will wax off the tan. And, for the record, it looks ridiculous.

57

What other kind of women like to wax? Strippers are a population that needs a good-looking bikini line since it is part of what can make them successful in their profession. So that is a whole other group I take care of. We have all kinds of strippers, though. We have the single moms who are making lots of money to provide for themselves and their kids. We have young girls dancing their way through college. And then we have the drug addicts who need to feed their habit. Those are the most fun (or should I say the most interesting) to do. Imagine a girl who pulls an all-nighter, comes in the next morning completely strung out, and proceeds to get naked so I can make her bald. It's a Saturday morning, and one of my most colorful strippers comes in so wired that you can almost feel the rush of tainted blood flowing through her veins. Or should I just say that it was alcohol and crack making its journey through her body. When I take her in the room, she drops her pants and takes a flying leap onto the table. She proceeds to lift both legs straight up in the air and kind of wiggles her toes a bit. Then she does a full straddle split and drops a leg on each side of the table and says, "Do me." So I did.

One of my guy clients asked me why strippers smell better down there. How the hell would I know? I try very hard to not use my sense of smell.

A lot of ladies feel funny keeping their socks or knee-highs on when they take their pants off. It may look awkward, but who cares? That's the least of my worries. You can even keep your shoes on if they are a pain to get off. The only area I need bare is your bush and your bottom.

We had a girl getting ready to hop onto the table when she asked me to wait a minute while she got something out of her purse. It was a sock. She got back on the table and shoved it in her mouth.

Women can be very particular when it comes to their lady parts. I have hand mirrors as well as full-length mirrors in each of my rooms so they can inspect my work. It is especially important when I leave some hair in the front area. They like to check how the shape looks with their physique. They also like to make sure I leave a symmetrical patch of hair down there, whether it is a triangle, landing strip, or letter. I had one lady ask me to leave the shape of a clam. I never understood why anyone would want anything fishy down there.

I have discovered that once a woman becomes hooked on a hair-free hoo-ha, it's hard for her to feel comfortable in a sexual situation when she is hairy. As I mentioned earlier, girls will often keep it hairy just so they won't sleep around. One of my college girls waxed all during her freshman year of college and slept around like crazy. Then she stopped coming in. My suspicion was that she may have contracted something and either was embarrassed to come in or just knew that she shouldn't. Sophomore year comes around and she stops by the salon for an eyebrow wax. I asked her if she needed anything else waxed and she said she had to stop being so promiscuous so she was going to stay hairy. She's a Russian girl and they can really grow some hair! So she went almost a year without a wax. One day she came in for a bikini and I teased her about sleeping around again. She said she had started swimming and her pubic hair grew too far down her leg so she had to at least get rid of any of the hair that stuck out of her suit.

When you see naked women all day, you come across all types of bodies. Along with a variety of body types, I see a variety of surgical procedures. Many women get breast augmentation surgery. Did you know that you could get a boob job by getting cut under the armpit, through the nipple, under the actual breast, or through the belly button? There is silicone and saline. I have seen a lot of saline breasts that have started leaking after just two years. When they leak, they pucker underneath the breast and it looks funny. Many times, the leakage is uneven. Then it looks really strange. One breast can be a noticeably different size than its partner. The average breast implants are supposed to be replaced every ten years, but, many times, they need to be replaced sooner because of the leakage. Some women get hair between their breasts or around the nipple and those are very easy areas to wax and are relatively painless. I know implants were a random mention, but breasts seem to complement this whole Brazilian discussion.

I have also seen breast reductions. This seems to be much more complicated. I have seen bodies that have been totally mutilated with incisions around the breast, on the stomach, and even around the waist areas. Many times this surgery leaves the woman with no feeling left in her breasts or in her nipples. Sometimes they even have to move the belly button. I have seen others with faint scars around the breast. Those aren't quite as bad. From what I have seen, it sounds like a much better idea to have them enhanced than reduced, at least as far as scars and sensations are concerned.

So what about liposuction? This is a fancy term for removing unwanted fat that won't go away no matter how much you diet or how thin you get. If the surgeon is any good, the procedure of removing fat should only leave a small incision and nobody should be able to tell that anything was done to alter the person's body. Our salon is close to several hospitals so we know a lot of surgical nurses. Many of our nurses have had liposuction and have shown me what the talented surgeons do and how the incisions should look. I have also seen some seriously botched-up surgeries that have not sucked out enough fat so that pockets of fat are left in the most peculiar spots. When someone has lost a lot of weight (like one hundred pounds or more), there is bound to be excess skin. There is a procedure where the surgeons cut an incision around the waist area from one side of the body to the other. One of my clients was left with a fairly large pocket of excess skin at the waist area on each side. It looks like the most peculiar set of love handles. I guess the moral of the story is: find a good surgeon, and ask for references.

I had a girl who routinely complained about her uneven labia skin. It was not really bad but she hated that the skin wasn't smooth and didn't resemble two perfectly uniform slices of a peach. I'll admit that it was definitely more difficult getting the hair out of the uneven area, but we just had to be more careful holding the skin taut. She often asked me if I thought it looked funny down there. I am not a huge admirer of the vagina and everybody is unique in that area, so it was hard for me to really say it didn't look normal. Who can say what a normal pussy should look like anyways? She even looked into having reconstructive labia surgery and we talked a lot about it. It is a surgical procedure that is more common than you think. On a side note, I think that would be an interesting profession. In fact, I could partner with a surgeon. I can't imagine a surgeon wanting to operate on a hairy surface. God, my possibilities are endless! Anyways, for my two cents worth, if you can afford it and it really bothers you, then go for it. She did.

You don't have to wait for a special occasion to get a wax, although I am convinced that sometimes it brings good luck. One lady hadn't been in for several months. When she did finally come in, her hair was long and thick. After she got waxed, she went camping for a weekend with her boyfriend. While away, her man proposed to her. One of the first things she asked him was, "Did you wait for me to get waxed before you proposed?" Although he didn't say yes, she is convinced he waited until she was properly groomed before he popped the question. Who knows if it mattered to him or if it was just a coincidence?

Another trend is to start getting waxed a few months before your man returns from the military. I love to be a part of a woman's preparation for her man's homecoming. Throughout my career, I have met many young men and women who were getting deployed for the second and third time. Some want to go; some dread it. In any case, I have new clients who want to do something special for their loved one's impending return. I usually recommend that they get waxed twice before their partner comes back so it is even smoother. I find that it usually takes the second wax for all the little hairs to be removed successfully, especially if the girls have been shaving. Just remember: the more you wax, the finer and thinner your hair comes in. It's a beautiful thing!

So whether a wax makes you feel cleaner, sexier, or more liberated, there are all types of women who are joining the experience—and it does not have to be a traumatic one. In fact, if you are truly traumatized, there are several products on the market that help numb the area before you get waxed. But, in my opinion, anybody can handle five to ten minutes of fast and thorough hair extraction, especially if it can lead to a month of genital freedom.

So I guess the answer to the question about what kind of woman waxes it all is simple.... Every kind.

Bald at Any Age

People often wonder if there is an age limit for getting waxed. All of my children have a fair amount of hair between their brows and I started waxing that area when they were seven. I have also waxed a young girl's arm at the age of nine. Younger skin tends to be more fragile so it depends on the body part and the person. In my opinion, if a child is embarrassed by his or her hair, it is more important to make them feel comfortable rather than worrying about if it is morally right to remove it or not because maybe they just don't seem quite old enough. I have always felt that since waxing is not a permanent solution, it shouldn't be such a big deal if a person is nine or ninety.

My oldest Brazilian client so far was seventy-five years old. That was challenging. Not only had the woman lost one hundred pounds, her skin was definitely older and more fragile. The combination of all three made it a more difficult wax than normal. And to make matters worse, her pubic hair was completely gray. Gray hair tends to be coarse and stubborn. I expected her skin to possibly bruise or bleed because of its inelasticity and age, and it didn't let me down. The whole service took longer than I would have liked but with some perseverance, I was able to make her completely bald. Now we had to see what her man thought of her new look. It turned out that he liked her Brazilian so much that, after her second time getting waxed by me, he began shaving her as part of their foreplay. How awesome is that? What I failed to mention is that this particular client is a nudist. She had seen pictures of what she referred to as a "smoothie" in some of her nudie magazines and she and her husband thought it could add some excitement to their sex life. Even though I am not a huge fan of shaving, I didn't mind that she started to shave. And even though I was much more careful waxing her aged, stretched skin, the actual procedure was just too traumatic for her.

It was also pretty cool for me to know that I added some new variety to their lovemaking. The best part of making this woman hair-free was her newfound sexual exploits. She told me during her first Brazilian appointment that she had never enjoyed receiving oral sex before and didn't understand what the big deal was. She enjoyed giving it, just not receiving. Well, at seventy-five years old, she now knew what she was missing! I have promised her a free Brazilian when she turns eighty just so I can say I waxed someone in their eighties!

My second-oldest client is sixty-nine years old. Appropriate number for our topic, wouldn't you say? She's a really neat lady who is dating a much younger guy. She had been going to another salon for a few years for what she thought was a Brazilian wax. I can't remember how she heard of us but when she came into the salon, I asked her what service she wanted, and she said a Brazilian. When she was on the table and I lifted her leg up and covered her lip with wax, she asked me, "Where do you think you are going with that popsicle stick!" So we had to quickly discuss what a Brazilian wax entails. I only had a limited time before I had to rip the strip off before her lip was permanently encased with blue wax. After my brief and succinct description of what hair I was removing, she was absolutely mortified. At this point I had to remove the lip hair because I had already applied the wax. The place she had been going to before me had just been removing the hair across her front and nothing down below. I am not sure if they were taking advantage of her because of her age or if there was just a misunder-standing about what a Brazilian really was. Either way, she was completed freaked out about where I was going with my stick. She didn't allow me to fully complete the service. After explaining to her how I would remove all of her rectal and pubic hair, she decided that she wanted me to omit her backside. I didn't want to do any more to make her feel uncomfortable. I explained to her the procedure we go through to clean off the wax and left the room.

All of the body waxing at Mark & M.E. takes place on the second and third floors of the salon (so nobody can hear the screaming!) and we have the place inundated with candles to create a more relaxing atmosphere. While I was outside of the room lighting some candles, I could hear her talking to herself. I could hear her say something to the effect of, "I cannot believe where she went with that popsicle stick. I just can't believe where she was putting that wax." She still comes to me. We just wax her bikini line now.

My mom told me when I first got into the wax business that you know you are old when your pubic hair goes gray. At the time, I was pretty disturbed by the thought of being gray down there. Now I have seen thousands of mounds of pubic hair, and, yes, it does go gray. That's another reason to get rid of it. If anything can make you feel old, that is it.

My husband found another solution to the problem of gray pubic hair. He buys Dixie Cups. When a client gets her gray hair dyed, he offers to send them home with a Dixie Cup full of their color so they can be a natural brunette or blonde everywhere. Pretty clever, wouldn't you say? Looks kind of funny when you are naked and have a beautiful brown mane on your head and a mound of white hair between your legs. Once again, problem solved.

It never occurred to me when I first started waxing that age might be an issue, but it has been. When I first started doing waxing, a sixteen-year-old came in for a bikini. (Remember that in 1994, people didn't know what Brazilians were and it wasn't part of our regular, everyday services at the salon.) She was dressed like a little girl and had pigtails in her hair. She asked me if it would be possible to wax her entire pubic area because her older boyfriend really liked her to look like a little girl. She said he was in college, which was very exciting to her, but he liked her to act and dress as young as possible. I don't know what you are thinking, but it sounded pretty creepy to me. Since then I have tried really hard not to pass judgment on any client who comes in to see me, but that day I couldn't help myself. I think her boyfriend sounded like a pedophile and the whole situation made me really uncomfortable. I gave her a bikini and sent her on her way.

So what is a good age to start waxing? As I said earlier, my children have dark hair and I started waxing between their brows at age seven. It is difficult being a wax technician and having children with unwanted facial hair. Children most definitely have more delicate skin and waxing can be more painful for them, so I wouldn't recommend waxing a young child unless he or she really wanted it. I have had several girls in the pre-teen age group who have been embarrassed by the hair on their arms. The first young girl whose arms I ever waxed told me that she was so embarrassed by her arm hair that even in the hottest part of summer she would wear long-sleeve shirts. When her mother told me about her daughter's insecurities regarding her arm hair, I felt so sad for her, especially knowing that I could safely remove her arm hair in a short amount of time.

One time, I had a kindergarten-age child come in with her mom. The mom told me that the kids in her daughter's class called her a monkey. She wanted me to wax her daughter's back, but I really felt that she was too young and it would have been too painful. This little girl really did have a lot of unwanted hair. After looking at

66

how heavily her hair grew on her back, I advised the mom to take her daughter to see a doctor and see if there was anything off with her hormone levels. Waxing would have not been worth it because she was so young and it really would have hurt her. She also had hair practically covering every square inch of her body. I couldn't see putting her through that much trauma when it wasn't a permanent solution to a pretty embarrassing situation. I also recommended that she try a topical depilatory hair remover as a temporary solution.

It is difficult to say whether a wax will be successful on a young girl until you try it. Often I will try a small spot to see if she can tolerate the pain that accompanies the procedure.

Sometimes the hair is so embarrassing for them that they will suck it up and try to endure any amount of pain that is caused by the wax. Other times, their skin is too delicate and it just isn't worth it.

If a young girl decides to go through with a wax, I usually give her two options. I can use large strips so the whole experience is over faster. I can also use small sections so each rip may be a little less painful. Letting her be part of the decision-making process gives her some control over the situation and definitely seems to be an effective tool.

A young teen came in one day and wanted a Brazilian. This was when I first got busy doing them and I had a lot of new people coming into the salon every week. I started chatting with her to try to make her more comfortable and didn't pay attention to her age. When I was about to put the wax on her, I set the stick back onto the edge of the tub and asked her how she got to the salon because she seemed way too young to be getting a Brazilian. She told me that her mother had brought her to Mark & M.E. and was well aware of what she was having waxed. I asked her if she was a dancer, runner, or gymnast, because those are the sports that often require some pubic grooming. She told me she just wanted it done. I completed the service, but she could barely take the pain. She was fourteen.

I had a high school senior successfully endure the wax (since it only took me six minutes to complete) but then her face turned freakishly white and when she stood up she said that she felt like she was going to pass out. She told me she needed to lie down on my floor. She proceeded to say that she even had issues having her finger poked by a needle and had passed out from that before. Unfortunately, the waxing procedure was far more traumatic than she anticipated. I gave her some hard candy because I have learned over the years that the sugar in candy can really help when someone is lightheaded, dizzy, or ready to crash. As a side note, I have bowls of candy all over the salon. Sometimes it is just good for the sake of distraction. Several women grab some candy before the wax to help prevent the lightheaded feeling that can accompany the service. Some people just like the distraction of chewing or sucking on a lollipop. I usually offer clients water when they are lightheaded, but this girl had her own bottle. I made sure that she drank some. Then I turned on the air conditioner and let her just lay there on the floor for almost thirty minutes. And, no, she didn't have pants on. She didn't want to crawl back on the massage table. So she stayed on the floor. She felt safer there. Fortunately, she had two friends in the room with her to keep her company while she recovered. She had been the driver to the salon but her friend drove her home since she was still shaky when she left.

I hate when waxing affects people so severely. And although I have found tricks to help them feel better, it can be quite unnerving.

I had a grown woman have the same response as the teen when she saw blood between her legs. She had used the product Retin-A on the front of her bikini area to help with the bumps and ingrown hairs. Now, if you know anything about Retin-A, it removes a layer or so of skin so waxing is absolutely forbidden. We have had a few scary incidents in the salon with people who have used this product and didn't let us know. One guy had used it on his shoulder area to control his acne. His skin was severely raw after I waxed it. It never occurred to me that anyone would put such an expensive product all over such a large area that isn't even exposed in the wintertime in Western New York. I also temporarily injured a woman's face who insisted she didn't use it. When she came back to the salon two days later, she admitted she used a little in conjunction with her acne medicine. It looked like I used a carrot peeler on her chin. It was horrible. Fortunately, it thoroughly healed.

Anyway, this woman faints when she sees blood, which I didn't know until I ripped a large strip from the front of her pubic area and saw the blood seep through the skin. When I told her we had a problem, she said she couldn't look at the area because she would faint. Just the thought of it bleeding made her crawl to the floor and assume a curled-up position until the unsteadiness passed. She stayed on the floor for almost twenty minutes then moved to the massage table for another twenty. She drank some of my Vitamin Water while curled on the floor and then munched on hard candy once she got back onto the table. It never occurred to me that anyone would ever use that kind of product on such a sensitive area. Live and learn.

Since I started this book in 2008, I have had more women in their sixties coming into the salon and getting Brazilians. They are much more comfortable with their bodies than the younger women and many of them are so forthcoming and so funny. A sixty-three-year-old woman came in and I asked her what her husband was going to say about her wax. She said he wouldn't notice. Four weeks later, I asked her if he noticed. She said, "Yeah." I asked her what he said. She said that he didn't say anything but she knew he liked it because she was getting a lot more oral. After a month, he wanted to know when she was going back to see me again. I guess he really did like it.

A first Brazilian wax often accompanies a monumental birthday. I've waxed countless women on their thirtieth, fortieth, and even fiftieth birthdays. It is perceived as an exciting and daring new adventure to mark their new decade. What a fun way to celebrate a special day!

Since we have such a variety of age groups that come to our salon, it has been a conscious decision on our part to put on appropriate music. Our local station that plays all slow songs made us tired and really didn't add to the upbeat feeling we like to maintain throughout the day. Believe it or not, waxing is fun and we try to foster a happy and upbeat environment. The current pop, hip hop, and rap music is just obnoxious and repetitive and too many clients found it objectionable. Jazz is too sleepy. We aren't big country fans. So we have settled for a station that tends to play a lot of oldies that people know and like to sing to. I often find myself singing or humming when I am working on a client. It tends to piss some people off, though. I can't help it. I look at vaginas all day and the music provides a nice distraction. One of my clients told me I should put on alternative, hard rock because it is loud and annoying and would be most suitable to the feeling when she got a Brazilian. I told her that "fork in the eye" music makes me angry and she wouldn't want an angry woman putting hot wax between her legs.

A girl came into the room and started to take her pants off when the music on the radio started playing, "Pussy cat, pussy cat, I love you." She started laughing hysterically. It was such an appropriate song to accompany the service. She was young and had never heard the song before which even made it funnier.

In my opinion, the answer to the question that I asked in the beginning is no. There should be no age limit to getting waxed. If a ten -minute service can make you feel better about yourself, then go for it.

Mastering a Woman's Mound

It has taken me years to perfect the Brazilian service and I am really proud of what I have accomplished. When I hear stories of a Brazilian taking over an hour, I know that I have figured out a technique that is so much more efficient and, believe it or not, so much more fun. I think it is time to share some of my secrets that have set me apart.

First, if you want to put your client at ease, you have to be chatty. At least that works for me. Silence, hot wax, pain, and an exposed vagina do not go together well. I love to talk and I love to wax; it's a great combination. I like to find out as much as possible about each client and I tend to remember facts about everyone. Pay attention and you'll be surprised what you remember about a person. On the other hand, I'm not as proficient with people's names. In fact, I suck at remembering names. I have always believed that it is more important for me to remember things about their lives and about them. In fact, I often surprise myself with all the things I remember about my clients.

I had a client about fifteen years ago that came in for her nails for her wedding. It was a fairy-tale romance. She was beautiful. He was beautiful. They both had good jobs. They bought a house. Life was idyllic. What she didn't know anything about was his cocaine addiction. Within the first year, he wiped out their savings, put them in debt, and became a whole new messed-up person. She divorced him, sold their house, moved back in with her folks, and had to start over from scratch. I saw her mother recently and asked about her by name (it was a different name that I actually remembered) because it was a story that was so sad and my heart ached for this girl. She got back on her feet and finally remarried and had a child. Hopefully, this really is the happy ending that she was hoping for the first time.

Don't be afraid to ask questions. It is really fun hearing about other people's lives. Kind of like a real-life soap opera, only better.

A good wax technician should also be fit. It takes a lot of strength and inertia to pull pubic hair out by the root. Although I work out regularly, I have to be really careful when I lift weights because my arms are always tired from doing so many people each week. I have some tendonitis in various parts as well as arthritis but I have found that massage, exercise, and occasional acupuncture keep me going. So even though I am fit, there are definitely some occupational hazards that can happen in this job because it is far more physical than people realize. For example, I herniated a disc in my neck waxing a forty-seven-year-old Italian lady who had never groomed that area. It was one scary mound of hair. The hair was very stubborn and I was having a difficult time getting it to come out. I was maneuvering myself in various positions trying to get better leverage, but I just couldn't get the hair to cooperate. And, to make matters worse, the hair was mostly gray, which is way more resistant to removal. I was in this incredibly awkward position and tried to pull a strip with as much gusto as possible and I felt the most excruciating stab at the base of my neck. It actually took my breath away and it took me a few minutes of pretending to fumble with my supplies to regain my composure. She never knew I hurt myself, and she never will. It wasn't her fault. It was an injury that was waiting to happen.

I thought about having surgery, but the surgeon said that if I continued waxing, I would probably end up herniating the discs around the one he fixed. So although it hurts, it hasn't slowed me down. I am still the fastest, most efficient ripper in town. Can't imagine if I wasn't fit. I'd be crippled.

A good technician needs to be energetic. The more energetic I feel, the more efficiently I can perform the service. And, trust me, being efficient is key. You wouldn't be happy if I spent forty-five minutes lingering over your lady parts. Ten minutes tops and you're as bald as a newborn. I have so many women that travel more than thirty minutes for me to wax them because I can perform the service so quickly. It's kind of an unwritten contract I have with thousands of women that I will have them bald and off the table in less than ten minutes, and, believe me, they appreciate it. It is not an experience that you want to dawdle over. I have heard countless stories of women who have gone to other salons and the service took forty-five to sixty minutes. It absolutely baffles me what could possibly take so long. Unless a happy ending accompanies the service, I would go elsewhere.

I tend to feed off the positive and negative energy of the women who enter the room. It saddens me how many women have suffered through divorce, mental and physical abuse, and a variety of really painful life experiences. It's hard not to feel people's sadness, stress, or heartache when they are sharing something important with you. One of my girls was on her third or fourth date with a guy and as they were fooling around, he aggressively took control and sodomized her. It was excruciatingly painful, and she had difficulty walking the next day. She told him to stop, but he was stronger than she was, so he didn't stop until he finished. She didn't feel like she could report him to anyone because she had slept with him before and had voluntarily gone to bed with him that time as well. I felt her pain and wanted to help her. I guess the only way I was able to help her was by listening. Sometimes the sadness is overwhelming. If you aren't the kind of person who gives a shit about another person's problems, then you won't be very good at this.

But it definitely makes my day even more fun when someone comes in full of positive energy. I get so excited when my clients get engaged or find out they are pregnant or have any life-altering experience that makes them happy. It is so wonderful to meet a woman who has a successful marriage, or who really loves her job, or who just enjoys life. The better you relate to the client and share her current state of mind, the more comfortable she will be taking her pants off in front of you.

If you are any good at waxing, then the whole procedure should take less than ten minutes. So if you plan to get to know your client and actually have a decent conversation, you have to talk fast. Casual conversation can't take place. There isn't enough time. Engaging in fun, energetic chatter is the way to go.

Don't be surprised where some women have hair. You need to be willing to wax everything. I have lots of ladies with hair on their fingers, toes, tip of the nose, and even nipples. You can't act surprised by hair in strange places. Just get rid of it. Imagine if you had hair on the tip of your nose? It's a bummer.

By the way, it is important to pay attention to more than just the area you are waxing. If a woman has a mustache or a big hair sticking out of a mole, offer to remove the hair. Often a client will forget that they wanted another body part waxed. I have waxed the cleavage area on many women over the years. It is also common for women to have hair on their nipples. Be available to take care of the miscellaneous stray hairs that can cause embarrassment. If they have a large area that needs to be waxed and you just don't have the time, have them set up an appointment for another wax. And pay attention to the elderly. Unfortunately, they tend to get a fair amount of unwanted hair on their face and it is up to us to make sure they are well-groomed.

Make sure you wear gloves. It seems obvious, but I have had clients who have been waxed at other salons tell me that they felt really uncomfortable when the technician didn't have gloves on. My preference is non-powdered black vinyl. They are the most comfortable. I also love the black because they look kind of mean.

When a client is lying on the table, the most common thing for them to look at is the ceiling. Not every woman will be comfortable looking you in the eye. So make sure your light or ceiling fan is not dirty. Your environment should always be as clean as possible. People are getting naked. Hair is being ripped off along with some dead skin. Some people are going to bleed. Keep a clean place. Not only will your clients notice, they will appreciate it.

Having a fan can be a good idea for the women who sweat a lot, but I personally find the moving air annoying. It tends to set the wax up too quickly. I also hate when the hair on my head moves. It distracts me. I had a professor who used to ride her bike to the salon on Saturday mornings for a leg wax. She lived pretty close by, but no matter what the temperature was outside she would sweat profusely as soon as she hopped up on the table. She felt sick if I didn't put the fan on a fairly high setting. It was pretty annoying to have the air move so quickly, but she would sweat so badly, I didn't have a choice. Only one of my rooms has a fan so we always used that room for her wax. It always took me a little longer to do her legs since I had a harder time working with the wax, but she was very interesting to talk to and our conversations always lasted the entire service.

Since I live in a cold climate, our heat is on quite a bit of the year. Even though you may not want your client to be cold when she undresses, as soon as you pull the first rip from her pussy, she will heat up. I have found that sixty-seven to sixty-eight degrees is as warm as I can keep the room. When women are in pain, they tend to sweat and if they get too hot, they will feel sick. And I have found that I will overheat as well if I come across a stubborn puss or a yucky one. So even though we like the number sixty-nine, it isn't a good temperature for your room. It is just too warm.

Make sure the area is well lit. Sometimes blond hair can be difficult to see and your clients will get pissed off if you don't get all of the hair. It's also easier to tweeze the stubborn hairs if you have better light. And when you have a lot of clients in one day, your eyes will get tired so good light is essential.

Women love to use their husbands' clippers to trim. Tell them to leave the clippers alone. So many times they clip the hair too short and it makes it coarse and prickly and difficult to wax. Offer to do the trimming when they come in for the service. This way you can control the length. Even a number-4 clipper attachment can cut some of the hair too short and then you, the technician, will get stuck tweezing. If the hair is long enough to braid, I trim it with scissors.

It's important to have good tweezers. I prefer needle-nosed tweezers because they get ingrown hairs out better. I sell pointed tweezers (which are similar but not as dangerous) and slanted. I don't sell the needle-nosed type anymore because too many women complained that they hurt themselves with them.

If you are going to wax someone, you should wax yourself. You need to know how it feels. I have waxed my whole body so I know exactly what every client is experiencing. There are parts I'm not keen on waxing on myself because it hurts too much. Interestingly enough, it's not the Brazilian.

You don't have to be funny to do this job and I have never thought of myself as such, but people do tend to laugh a lot in my wax rooms. I do think my job is funny. Spread hot wax with a popsicle stick all over a woman's vagina and rip as hard and as fast as you can. Pretty funny. The weird thing is that I hurt people all day long and they just keep coming back. There has to be something positive about the experience aside from kick-ass sex once the redness and throbbing pass. I had a girl with a J-Lo butt laughing so hard one day that her butt cheeks were flapping together and since I had just applied the wax in her crack, her butt cheeks were pretty glued together. I am often reminded of the Go-Go's song "Our Lips Are Sealed." When this girl was laughing and her butt was slapping, I thought I was going to wet my pants. And, believe me, after three kids, leakage is a definite possibility.

That reminds me: they have disposable panties if you are more comfortable using them on clients. I think they are a pain in the ass and get in the way. I had a case of them and after ten years I threw the whole case out. And if you aren't comfortable looking at a vagina, do something else for a living.

Yoga moves work best for me. I have the clients get in a "one-legged happy baby." The position is also called a "dead bug." It makes it easier to get the labia and part of the rectum. And the clients who are really flexible are my favorite. It's just easier to get to their parts. I never have them do a "full happy baby" with both legs up, however. It's a degrading move and not necessary. It also increases the chance of the woman farting on you.

You need to be positive. Nobody wants someone with a negative slug type of personality examining their most precious parts with a puss on their face. Pun intended. My parents were two of the most positive people I ever met. They worked in a business out of our home so their influence was extremely powerful. They were also very happy together and I have tried to live by their example. My dad's life was cut short, so although it may sound cliché, I really do try to live life to the fullest. I love my family, my job, my life. Being happy is a good thing. Moral of the story: find a career that makes you happy.

You need to look good, too. If you work in the beauty industry, there are certain expectations from the clients. You should have good hair, wear makeup, and have polished nails. When I counsel prospective cosmetology students about the business, I always include a discussion about eating healthy, exercising regularly, and getting adequate rest. We should set an example and I think all people in this business should make an effort to look their best—although I have to admit that no matter how much makeup you wear or how stylish your hair is, the women I find most beautiful tend to be the ones who are happy. Go figure.

You really need to think about how you want things done. Every service performed at our salon is done in a way that my husband and I would want the service performed on us. For example, nobody gets on his or her hands and knees to get their butt crack waxed. Doggie style should not be a public position. That is the way most technicians do it and it has never seemed logistically plausible to me. Demeaning, definitely. Embarrassing, yep. Ridiculous, absolutely. So no client ever gets on their hands and knees at our place. Doggie style should be left in the privacy of the bedroom.

Think about what you are doing. When we give a facial, for example, we don't leave the room when a masque is on. We rub your hands, feet, and head. We try to do something nice to pass the time. I hate when aestheticians leave the room during a facial. It makes me anxious. And what if the product they put on my face started to burn since my skin is so sensitive? Would I start yelling for someone to come take it off of me? So I don't leave. One time I got a facial at a local salon that specialized in skin care. During the treatment, the girl left the room for twenty minutes. I was losing my mind. When she came back, she reeked of cigarette smoke. I couldn't have been more annoyed.

You can't act surprised or grossed out when something unpleasant happens. I lifted up a leg to rip the inner thigh of a forty-something

78

woman when a long string of gas poured out of her. It was long, smelly, and loud enough that there was no way either of us could pretend it didn't happen. She said she tends to be gassier now that she is older. Gee, thanks.

It is important to make the client as comfortable as possible and keep the narrative light and fun. Often when a woman's vagina looks red or sore and they are excited about having sex with their new look, I worry that it will be painful if they don't allow their body to heal. So I offer the best advice I can. I often tell my ladies to tell their partner that they need to be gentle with them after they have been waxed. I also advise them to tell their partner that it would be beneficial to have them lick their wounds. Lubrication after a wax is a must if you plan to engage in sexual activity that same day.

Since our salon is near so many colleges, our client turnover is really high. Occasionally, I have a client who will decide that she wants to learn how to wax herself. I have no problem teaching someone how to wax, but I have discovered that it can be logistically difficult with some body types to get to the entire area successfully. Other women find out that they just cannot do it because it hurts and it is hard to hurt yourself. One of my married ladies moved down South and called me in a panic on a busy Saturday afternoon. She was in the process of giving herself a Brazilian and couldn't get the wax off of her lips. It hardened against her body and she couldn't get it to adhere to the strip. She was totally freaking out. She asked me to go to a quiet part of the salon to help walk her through it. My first bit of advice was for her to ask her husband for help, but she said he would probably faint. That wouldn't help. So I walked her through the steps of trying to reheat the wax stuck on her body and offered her the courage and direction she needed to successfully wax her bikini area.

You may come across someone who gets hives. It seems that sometimes the trauma to the skin can cause hives. I have seen them on the brows, upper lip, and bikini area. They look like a round, raised, white spot and tend to surface immediately. I have found that taking Benadryl before a wax can help prevent an outbreak of hives. Some people will get them randomly. Other clients stop getting them once they have been a waxed a few times and their skin gets more accustomed to the procedure. It's a random reaction that I haven't been able to pinpoint to an exact cause. I've just learned to be a little less freaked out when I see them.

When you rip a large strip off of a woman who has long, dark hair, it can be quite astounding how it looks on the strip. I try to rip as large a strip as possible to make the service go more quickly. Sometimes I am flabbergasted not only by the amount of hair on the strip but the size of the roots at the end of the hair. Women are usually disgusted by how their hair looks. I find it fascinating. One client thought the massive amount of long, dark hair on the strip looked like a Chia Pet. It did.

Does it matter if your client is a virgin? No, of course it doesn't. A seventeen-year-old virgin came in with a few friends for her first wax and was petrified for me to see her naked. I tried to assure her that it was no big deal but she was terrified. She asked for a towel to cover her pubic area. There are salons out there that provide modesty towels. If it makes the client feel more comfortable, I guess it could be a good idea. For me, I find a towel gets in the way. You want to be bald in five minutes? Get naked and let me do my job. This girl proceeded to giggle through the entire service. She continued to use the modesty towels for months. One day, she said she didn't need the towel anymore and really wanted me to make sure I was extra thorough removing all her hair. Oh, yeah, she had gotten laid.

"But I shaved three days ago. What do you mean it isn't long enough?" Are you kidding me! I have women every week who come in with hair that is freshly shaved and expect it all to wax off cleanly and smoothly. You need to tell people on the phone to grow their hair or they are wasting their time and money. To me, it seems obvious that it needs to be long enough to wax off well, but that has been a constant poor assumption on my part for years now. So this is the deal: I don't care how hairy you think you are or how fast you think your hair grows, you need at least two weeks' growth before getting a decent wax. Yes, sometimes I can get a fairly good wax after seven to ten days, but not very often. Clients need to be patient and grow it.

And, for the record, you shouldn't decide to wax for a living just for the money. You have to enjoy doing it. If you don't love it, the client will know. Many cosmetology students decide they want to wax because they think they can make a lot of money doing it. A grossed-out expression toward a nasty puss or a dirty rectum will not make the client comfortable with the service. Situations like that are just part of it. Yes, the money can be good. But, trust me, that cannot be your motivation.

It is supposed to be taboo to discuss religion or politics in the salon. Although I agree that in a busy, public area one should be cautious about open discussion, that rule totally does not apply to the wax room. Nothing is off limits. Politics and religion are some of the safer and less shocking topics. I know several women who have been raped, sodomized, and beaten. I am glad when a woman feels safe enough to share their horrific tales with me. I know that it can be cathartic for some people. It saddens me to hear about all of the abuse from husbands, boyfriends, parents, siblings, relatives, and strangers. I've had girls who have come in trashed, stoned, and high on crack. There is talk of parties and orgies. We talk about sex. And more sex. And vibrators. And lubricants. And deviance. Lots and lots of deviance. The wax room provides a fascinating forum to discuss anything and everything. That is what makes my occupation so exciting. I thrive on the stories and the energy and the disclosures.

Sounds intriguing, doesn't it? In fact, you are thinking about a career change, aren't you?

No matter what the age of the client, everyone has his or her own unique way of dealing with the experience. Just because a woman has had children doesn't mean she will be able to deal with it any better than a young teen. There are all sorts of coping mechanisms that my clients use to deal with it. People seem to think that taking prescription drugs helps, but, in my experience, it really lowers your resistance. Ibuprofen is probably the most common drug of choice, but taking more than two can increase your risk of bruising. Painkillers, like Vicoden, are another fairly common drug that my clients seem to have on hand, but they don't seem to help. Xanax is always an interesting drug to take. Clients who take Xanax just seem totally stoned and at least can't fight me too much. I've always enjoyed this girl who does a couple of shots of Tequila before she comes in. What really cracks me up is that she usually makes her appointment before noon. Every time I wax her she smells like a brewery and laughs gregariously. Now Imitrex, for migraines, is one drug I always avoid. It tends to make you overly sensitive, even to the touch. I had a lady start crying and shaking because one little rip felt like I was branding her. So the best advice I can give a new client is to suck it up, come in sober, and let me do my job.

A girl once came in hung over and stoned. Not a smart combination. Alcohol tends to thin the blood and bruising can happen much more easily. Also, people who have had a lot to drink tend to have slept poorly and their resistance is lower. So let's be hung over, get high, and go for your first Brazilian wax! I'll never forget this girl. She was a tall, slender, and dark-haired girl who bartended at a local restaurant that my husband and I frequent. When her leg was up in the air, I ripped her one lip in one quick swipe. She yelled, "Holy fuck," kicked me in the head, rolled away from me, and fell off the table. Funny thing was that she never realized that she kicked me. She was more concerned that she had yelled an obscenity so loudly. I couldn't believe she had kicked me in the head. She was a tall girl so her leg clocked me in the back of the head against the skull. It really didn't hurt. I was just startled. After that, she was all discombobulated and the rest of the wax was really difficult because she was fighting me.

Falling off the bed isn't as uncommon as you think. One girl got a gift certificate from a friend to get a waxed. She even brought her friend into the room for moral support. Having friends in the room, by the way, is not uncommon. I actually encourage it. The more, the merrier. The girl getting waxed was a black girl and black hair can be more difficult to wax. She was really nervous and had psyched herself out even before she had removed her jeans. Her girlfriend sat in a chair near the head of the massage table and was hysterically laughing before we even started. I started off doing really small strips because she was wiggling all around and I didn't want to bruise her. Her legs were flailing all over the table and I had to use my body as leverage to keep her leg up. I also used my body as leverage to keep her from rolling away from me. When her leg that was furthest from my body was in the air, I wasn't able to hang on to her as well so when I ripped the inside of her buttocks, she rolled away from me and ended up in a heap on the floor. Her girlfriend was laughing so hard she was snorting. Getting her back onto the table was no easy feat.

Over the years, whenever a woman has fallen off the table, she has always fallen away from me. That is, until recently. I had a girl's leg in the air that was closest to me, and when I pulled the strip, she rolled toward me and fell into my arms. Fortunately, she was not a very big girl and I was able to catch her.

I taught a private wax class to two girls who worked at a friend's salon. They brought in models, which is totally necessary in a class.

It must be a hands-on experience. You cannot learn by just watching. The one technician was easygoing, likeable, and eager to learn. The other girl was young, arrogant, and annoying. She acted like she knew it all. Not only was she resistant to my advice and experience, she was combative when I told her that the wax she wanted to use for Brazilians was not a good choice. I knew that the wax she wanted to use didn't work on coarse pubic hair. It was obvious to me in the first ten minutes that she would never be a successful wax technician. Currently, she is cutting hair for a living.

So what happens when you see a client in public? After I wax someone and leave the room, I like to put their pubic area out of my mind. It really isn't something I want to dwell on. It is pretty funny, however, how differently people respond to me when they see me out. When I am at the gym, people often don't even recognize me. I tend to wear a baseball hat and have no makeup on, so I suppose I may be a little harder to recognize. When I see a girl out with her guy, the guys are either psyched to meet me or overtly embarrassed. The best encounter I ever had seeing a client out of the salon involved my call for jury duty. I had the flu and couldn't have looked any worse. When I walked into the courtroom with seventy-five other people, I looked at the district attorney and she was one of my regular clients. She did a double-take, got the strangest expression on her face, and then looked down and started texting. It turns out she was texting her boyfriend and telling him that I was on her jury. He wanted to know if I was cool. She said "yeah" but was really surprised to see me. I was one of the first twenty-one people called to sit in the jury box. The first question the judge asked is if any of us knew either of the attorneys or the defendant. I was the only one who raised my hand. He asked whom I knew. Well, I only knew her nickname so I just pointed in her direction and said, "I know her." When he asked how I knew her, I had to stifle a laugh. (Couldn't be a stranger way of knowing someone.) I told him she was a client of mine at my beauty salon. He asked me if we ever talked about any of her cases. I said no. What I didn't tell him was that the last time she had been at the shop, we talked about this gay porn shop in town that sold awesome sexual lubricants. I was dismissed from serving.

So if you really think that making women bald for a living is your calling, good luck. You are going to need a strong stomach, an open mind, and an agreeable demeanor. This career is both physical and emotional. It is also exhilarating and exhausting. And I love it.

Crazy Shit People Tell Me

In the summer of 2008, I decided that I should just start jotting down the weird stuff people tell me because a lot of it is funny, and, occasionally, it renders me speechless. For example, I had a woman tell me her dog liked to chew on the crotch of her panties. She thought it was adorable. She was having marital problems and when her husband asked her, "What the hell is the dog doing?" she told him that the dog liked chewing on her panties even if he wasn't interested in that part of her anatomy. She also told him that the dog probably liked it so much because other men had told her that she had lovely smelling lady parts.

Most people are baffled by what I do for a living. I know it can be hard to visualize the process of the service I provide unless you have had it done. My own mother cannot believe that women willingly come into my rooms, take off their pants with no hesitation, and jump on the table so I can do my thing. So I decided that it might be fun to take you through a typical day at Mark & M.E.

10:00 AM: A girl asked me to leave a patch of hair in the front that looked like mistletoe. At first, I didn't put together the time of year with the request. So I asked her, "Why a mistletoe?" She said that she was going to ask her boyfriend to kiss her under the mistletoe.

10:10 AM: The next girl wanted a Wheat Thin patch left on the front. No problem. Making that area edible is my specialty.

87

10:15 AM: A woman said her husband told her that she needed to take care of her "enchanted forest." I told her there was nothing enchanting about her mound of long, nasty pubic hair.

10:30 AM: Three college students made a group dare and came in for their first-ever Brazilians. The first two were moaning and groaning but made it through. The third girl wanted to chicken out but neither her friends nor I would let her take a pass. I was halfway through the wax when she told me she hated me. I just laughed and told her that in fifteen years I had been told that many times. Then she told me she *really* hated me in a quiet, growling voice. She proceeded to tell me that what I was doing to her was making her really angry. In fact, she planned to punch something when the service was over. It was so funny that her one friend had to leave the room to go pee because she thought she was going to wet herself. When I was cashing her out, she apologized for telling me that she hated me because she really didn't and she thought she'd be coming back next month. I told her I wasn't offended and I felt confident that the next visit would be easier on her.

11:00 AM: I waxed a college student who giggled incessantly from the moment she climbed on the table. I asked her if she giggled like that during sex. She said, "Only if his penis is small."

11:15 AM: A client entered the waiting room. I asked her if she was getting ripped. She said, "Yeah." I asked her if she needed to use the restroom. She slowly said, "No, girl. Let's get this over with." As we were walking toward the stairwell to go upstairs, she said, "Oh, Lord, I remember this hallway." A few more steps and she mumbled, "Oh, Lord, I remember walking up these stairs." Then she started slowly and deliberately stomping up the stairs like she was being sent to death row. It was then when she said, "This feels like the walk of shame." I knew I had a struggle ahead of me.

11:30 AM: When I walked into the waiting room to get my next client, she asked me if I was really okay with it being corked. It took me a minute to figure out what she was referring to. "Yeah, I am okay with it." I am the queen of moving tampon strings.

11:45 AM: Brazilians are very liberating and I think this new feeling often leads to more liberating comments and discussions, especially from women who tend to be on the conservative or introverted side. In all these years, there have been very few topics that ended abruptly or uncomfortably. This forty-year-old client got very defensive and weird when I asked to wax her backside. A friend of hers was in the room and they were incredibly open about their sex lives, but when I wanted her to roll on her side, she became very angry, like I was performing an inappropriate and violating service on her. She got really pissed that I wanted to complete the service and the entire mood in the room changed. She made me feel very uncomfortable, which is not normal for me at all. It was one of the few times that I wanted to run out of the room and not finish the service. Although the rest of the time I was in the room with her was terribly awkward, she continued to come to me until she moved out of town. I imagine she had been abused in that area. I would never want someone to feel uncomfortable or scared and I never offered to do that area on her again. It just didn't make sense because both women shared intimate details about their sex lives almost every time they came in more detail then I needed to know. All I know for sure is that this was an area that was definitely off limits.

High Noon: I've become a little more cantankerous as I've gotten older when a client isn't cooperative. Sorry, ladies, but my back hurts and my arms get tired. I could not get this woman with this biggest booty you have ever seen to spread her cheeks apart. She was very dark-skinned and I felt like I was entering a dark cavern with a blindfold on. I wasn't strong enough to lift her left cheek and it seemed like I was digging to China trying to find her rectum. After several times of asking her politely to lift her cheek higher, I loudly told her to "spread 'em like you mean it!" What I didn't realize until I heard laughter nearby was that there were three women in my waiting room waiting to be waxed who heard me. The client did lift the cheek higher but started laughing really hard as well. When someone lifts her cheek and starts to laugh, there is something common that happens. She passed a symphony of gas. Will I ever learn?

12:15 PM: This client told me that her man couldn't get an erection even with the little blue pill. I told her I'd get a new man.

12:20 PM: Three women traveled from almost an hour away to get waxed at our salon. It has become more common for people to travel that far because I am just that much faster than the average technician. And I have to interject once again how truly humbled I am by the kind of dedication that women show to me. Two of the women had been to the salon before and loved the newfound freedom that accompanies a Brazilian wax. They were determined to get all of their friends to join the new craze. Whenever I first meet a new client, I ask them a zillion questions to try to get to know them and to put them at ease. It is also how I try to distract them from what I am doing to them. As we were talking, a hygiene discussion ensued and she assured me that she power-washed her parts that morning. I thanked her profusely and told her that I wished every client that came to me was as considerate. After I met her, I entertained the thought of using that expression as the title of this book. *Power-Wash Your Pussy* has a nice ring to it.

12:45 PM: I actually have a minute to grab something to eat. My days fly by and if I don't pay attention, many hours will pass and I'll forget to eat. There are also times that the last thing I want to do is put something in my mouth because of an unpleasant encounter. I have mentioned to several of my regular clients that I was writing a book. I have also mentioned that my hygiene chapter seems to be the longest. Since then, many of my clients are being much more conscientious about their own personal hygiene. I should have started a book long ago.

1:00 PM: Have you ever seen the scene in the movie *Home Alone* when the main character uses after-shave lotion on his face for the first time and screams? That is what happened to this client when she used the hand sanitizer on her puss instead of her hands when she was cleaning up.

1:15 PM: The boyfriend came in to watch this girl get a wax. She was a pretty big girl and they actually met on a dating website for guys who like big girls. While I was waxing her, he told me that nothing is better then burying your face in a fat woman's pussy. It was hard not be amused by his candor. So I looked at her and said, "lucky you!"

1:30 PM: The next client had a boyfriend drop her off to get a wax. As she was getting out of the car, he asked her to tell me to "be careful" when I wax it "because it's precious territory down there."

1:45 PM: I have a very random thought process that is continual and non-stop. It's probably pretty obvious by the way I write and also explains why I sleep like shit. I just remembered the Saturday after Thanksgiving 2009. I think everybody had intercourse either that Friday night or on Saturday morning since it was a holiday. My first three appointments that day all reeked of sex. Ugh.

1:50 PM: A girl called the salon and told us she went somewhere else to get waxed since she moved several hours away. Not only did the service last an hour, the technician had the client hold a popsicle stick over the opening of her vagina. No, that wouldn't be awkward.

2:00 PM: This client has a bunch of mentally handicapped foster children living with her. She is an amazing lady who has dedicated her life to kids with special needs. She doesn't come to the salon often because she has a hard time finding people to stay with the kids. When she does come in, she likes to tell me that our salon is

91

her oasis. It always seems ironic when she says that to me since she doesn't come in for a luxurious service like a facial or body wrap. She comes in for a Brazilian. If a waxing constitutes an oasis in her mind, I cannot even imagine what life is like for her.

2:15 PM: Time for another random thought and the chance to pee. I am not a fan of hard wax. There are too many things that can go wrong if you don't do it just right. I like the efficiency of soft wax. I also like the barrier of using strips between my hands and your vagina. My best friend lives far from me. She went somewhere in her hometown to get a Brazilian. The woman used hard wax. It wouldn't dry. The technician had to hold a small fan between my friend's legs to get the wax to harden. God, I wish I could have been there to see that!

2:20 PM: This client had to find the right piece of candy before I waxed her. Although I have candy bowls all over the salon as a reward or a distraction, please remember how easy hard candy is to choke on when you are under duress.

2:30 PM: This single mom couldn't afford to get waxed anymore so she started shaving. She developed two ingrown hairs that became swollen and painful. When she went to the doctor, he told her to go directly to the emergency room. She had developed abscesses where the ingrown hairs were and the infection was spreading through her body. They had to put her on IV antibiotics overnight. Then she was sent home with mega-doses of antibiotics to take orally for ten more days. She decided that she would start waxing again regardless of the cost because now it had become a medical necessity for her. I told you shaving was evil.

2:40 PM: During the winter when there was snow on the ground, this client was asked by her fiancé to mow the lawn. She asked him what the heck he was talking about since it was normally his job to mow the lawn and, besides, there was snow on the ground. He told her that wasn't the lawn he was referring to.

2:45 PM: I got a really good laugh from this fifty-two-year-old woman who told me that I had sealed her shut and she wouldn't be able to pee for a week. When I started to wax her backside, she yelled out, "Now I won't be able to take a shit for a month!" She was worried that I would need the room for another wax because she was convinced that it would take forever to unstick all her parts. Unfortunately, being sticky is one of the negative side effects of waxing. I have discovered that oil will remove the sticky residue better than any fancy wax removal product sold on the market. No catheter or colostomy bag needed. I am happy to say she was able to unstick her parts.

2:55 PM: Another random thought…I was trained to be an educator for a certain wax company and they sold a product to remove the wax residue, but I have found that almost any non-fragrant oil will remove the stickiness even better without all the added fragrance that can cause vaginal irritations. When you are dealing with dozens of women each week, you can never gauge how many will be irritated from any given fragrance or extra chemical. It has always seemed in my best interest to be as safe as possible with the products used on such a delicate area. Enough advice. It's boring.

2:56 PM: Here is something that is not boring. Say the word "Twat." C'mon, say it aloud. Isn't it fun to say?

3:00 PM: I waxed the genitalia of a man who begged me not to finish the procedure. I had waxed his wife earlier that day and told him if she could do it, so could he. So I finished. I always do. When he was cashing out, he asked me if waxing was like childbirth and you forget the pain. Who is he kidding? Natural childbirth is a lot harder then getting a Brazilian. And how the hell would he know what childbirth was like? Believe me, you don't forget.

3:10 PM: This girl was really worried that I was going to cause damage down there because of the speed and gusto that I use when I ripping the hair off her. It's funny because, in some ways, the puss is delicate. In other ways, I can rip the shit out of it and it's no big deal. Just depends on the person and the puss.

3:15 PM: I started a blog to showcase my work, to get more exposure, and to give my clients a sample of how I write. I figured it would be a good preface to this book. This client told me that I better not write anything about her fat ass in my blog. Whoops, I just did. My blog is called "Hose Down Your Hoo-ha." Once you've read my chapter on hygiene, you probably understand the title a little better.

3:30 PM: I was thoroughly flattered when I heard that two of my regular clients were traveling to Baltimore with a friend who had never been waxed and they started talking about me. As they were driving, the one girl pulled up my blog on her iPhone and started reading it aloud. Listening to what I write about and how I write made the new girl feel more comfortable trying me out. She figured she couldn't be the worst-case scenario and she also thought she'd be comfortable having me do it. When we met, she told me the story. She also told me that she hoped she never made it on the blog site. I put this story on the next morning. The last client the following day was the girl who read her the blog. I told her that I felt compelled to write about their story because it really made me feel good. She was so excited. She couldn't wait to call her friend and tell her I wrote about them.

3:45 PM: I had two young girls say that getting waxed is only uncomfortable if you make it that way. And they were referring to both them and me. It doesn't make me feel weird at all and they love coming to the salon. I thought it was pretty insightful, wouldn't you say?

4:00 PM: A man called his wife a "Sasquatch." She called me and made this appointment.

4:10 PM: Another man threw a fifty-dollar bill at his wife. She also called me and made this appointment.

4:15 PM: This girl asked her friend, who was a licensed cosmetologist, if she'd give her a Brazilian. The friend said she'd rather give her a kidney.

4:20 PM: When this woman was thinking about finding a salon to get a Brazilian, her boyfriend told her that his ex-wife goes to Mark & M.E.

4:28 PM: Another random thought after looking at the last woman's hairy legs. Clients get so embarrassed when they come in with their legs unshaved. Believe me, that's not where I am looking. I could care less if your legs are shaved. It's much more important that your cootch is clean. Anyway, I am much more likely to notice your chipped polish on your hands or feet when you are holding your leg up. I was a nail technician first, so I tend to notice polish. I almost always notice are engagement rings since I stand on the person's left side and their left hand is in my face when they hang on to their hamstring.

4:30 PM: This woman was funny. When I finished waxing her, she yelled, "A man must have invented that sadistic shit!"

4:40 PM: This woman said she knew it was time to come in for a wax because her ass hair was getting tangled in her thong.

4:45 PM: I have been called all sorts of names over the years. This woman called me a bitch at the top of her lungs. I laughed because she had just told me that her husband had mocked her because her hair was so long and he wondered if the '70s porn star look was back. Yes, it can be more painful when it is long and dense. And, no, I don't like trimming your bush. I do think being called a porn star is pretty amusing. Being called a bitch, however, was nothing new. Being called a devil, however, is an isolated incident. A girl just blurted out, "You are the devil." I just kept going and chatted away like I always do. It takes more than a little name-calling to slow me down. When I turned her on her side to do the final rip, she informed me that my devil status was waning.

5:00 PM: A woman with female medical problems in need of a hysterectomy decided to try me out for a wax. Her first experience at another salon lasted forty-five minutes and she heard I was much more expedient. I had to be very careful with her skin since she was unwell in that area and women in need of hysterectomies tend to bruise more easily. She got some slight bruising, but I was very happy with how it turned out. And she was very happy that it took less than ten minutes. The next day she went to her gynecologist for her pre-operative exam. He noticed the bruising. He asked her who gave her a Brazilian. She told him that Zorro did. He told her to tell Zorro to slow down.

5:15 PM: This woman, who was in her fifties, brought her fourteen-year-old granddaughter in the room while she got waxed. That was awkward.

5:28 PM: By the way, if you pee after a wax and it sprays across the room, spend more time cleaning up after I finish.

5:30 PM: This client is married and is having a pretty intense affair with a married man. She told me that he wanted to fuck her in the ass, so she let him. Afterward, she started crying because it hurt so badly. He said he was sorry. She said it was okay. And then he said, "No, I am sorry because I really liked it."

5:40 PM: Crazy sex can lead to sore muscles. I get that. But when this woman told me that she could barely laugh because her stomach was so sore from having six orgasms in one night, I was impressed. I have so many clients that are ambivalent about sex; it surprises me that they even bother to get Brazilians. So I must admit that this woman's confession made me happy.

5:45 PM: There are a lot of men and women who make references to the 1970s when describing their hairy bushes. I always find it an amusing description, especially if you watch some porn from that era and see that there is some truth in it. What it really makes me think of is that I could have made a fortune in that decade. This girl had a 70's bush.

5:50 PM: This was a high school student who was bi-polar and liked to cut herself. I noticed the scars on her legs and she said she cut herself there so no one would notice. She usually did it before school. Her mother worked as a custodian at a psychiatric hospital and she decided that her daughter didn't need to be medicated. I didn't realize custodians were qualified to make that decision. The girl told me even though she didn't feel like she needed to be medicated, she still liked cutting herself but had it under control. One visit I asked her when the last time she cut herself was. It had been about a week. She said she really enjoyed re-piercing the skin above her nipples. I think that sounds more painful then a Brazilian.

6:08 PM: A lot of clients assume I am into sado-masochistic behavior. I'm not! I know it seems ruthless when I am ripping as fast as possible with a big smile on my face all the while knowing how badly I am hurting you. But you need to understand that I am really being considerate. The faster I rip, the less it hurts and the quicker I finish. And, not for nothing, I need to keep a sense of humor. By now, that should be pretty easy to understand.

6:10 PM: I was really flattered when two separate personal trainers came into the shop wearing one of my personalized shirts. This one was the second one this week. The shirts say "Get Ripped" and each of the girls had worn their shirts to work. I can't beat that type of advertising. Although the "Get Ripped" expression sounds callous, it is just the phrase I started using years ago. When you wax any body part, it often sounds like you are ripping paper. So it seems like an appropriate analogy. Besides, the phrase can have so many other connotations; I just love it.

I actually started making shirts just on a whim and they have been a huge hit. Some people buy them and others receive them from us for free when they send us a referral. My first shirts said "Been to Brazil." One night I was at a bar and was wearing that shirt and a man approached me and asked me if I was from Brazil because he really liked women from other places. Yuck. We also have a shirt that says "Mark & M.E. Sexy and Hair-Free." Liked the rhyme. Our baseball shirts say "Real Women..." on the front and "Wax It All" on the back. These are baby pink and white. They are very cute. We had "Team Brazil" shirts made up for the Olympics. The most popular shirt says "Brazilian Boot Camp." They are in army fatigue colors and can be seen on all ages of women all over town. I think this is a fun way to advertise. When my daughter was about fifteen years old, she called me from the mall. She was all excited because she saw a girl with one of my "Brazilian Boot Camp" shirts on and army fatigue pants. She wanted to tell me how cute this girl looked. So I asked her if she said hi to the girl and told her that she was my daughter. Her response: "Ewww, NO!"

Thank goodness my children are getting older so they don't have to be embarrassed by their mom's career. Well, I can only hope.

6:15 PM: A bachelorette party came in for a group wax. One girl giggled throughout the service, another was really quiet and wouldn't talk at all, the third girl swore a lot, and a final girl was loud and making strange moaning noises. Suddenly it occurred to me that maybe this is what the girls were like when they had sex. So I asked the group, "Is this how you ladies sound when you're doing it?" They all started laughing hysterically. I guess they all lived in a house together at one point in college and they knew intimate things about each other. It appears I figured out some of their secrets.

6:40 PM: When this client, who was new, was cleaning up after her wax, she said she was so excited by how smooth it was that she wished she could kiss it. She said that if she could reach it, she wouldn't need her boyfriend.

6:50 PM: A woman in her forties came in with her sisters for a wax. The sisters had already been to me before and knew it wasn't a big deal. She was so nervous that she kept saying that she should have had a drink before she came to the salon. My husband overheard her. He went into the kitchen and brought out an airplane-size bottle of alcohol for her to drink. When I took her upstairs, she made me stop halfway through the service so she could sit up and finish the little bottle.

7:00 PM: I love to learn about other people's lives and one of the best aspects about working with the public is all of the interesting people we meet. For example, we have gay couples that have had children. It always fascinates me as to the logistics of who decides to carry the baby and how they choose their donors. While it might seem pushy and forward, I have my genuine interest in the lives of the people I interact with all day. And I can't help but ask questions. So I asked this girl how they decided who would actually have the baby. She said they used the one partner's brother as the donor so the other partner carried the baby. In fact, they have two children with the help of their very special uncle. Now that is cool.

Speaking of uncles...one of my district attorneys told me one of the most disturbing stories. She works for children who are abused. She had a nine- and twelve-year-old pair of sisters that were sent by their mother to their uncle when they were bad. Instead of washing their mouth out with soap, he would put soap on his penis and have them suck it off. I applaud my clients for the work they do. I can't imagine working with offenders like that. Some of the stories I hear are so sick. Happy to say this particular uncle is in jail.

7:10 PM: A woman came in and she acted very solemn. She told me her divorce was finalized that day and she was having a really hard time with it. She had two children with her husband but it turned out that he was gay. In this situation, no matter how much she loved him and wanted to protect their vows, she could not change the fact that he was a homosexual. Her sadness and anger were so profound. It really infuriated her that her husband wanted to fuck men. She was trying to move on, but trust was a huge issue for her. This is not an isolated story. I had another client years ago who thought she was happily married. Their biggest marital problem was trying to get pregnant. When she finally did and successfully had their child, he left her for another man. She felt so betrayed. But he told her that he needed to be true to himself and only stuck around long enough to make sure she got her baby.

7:15 PM: Unfortunately, I hear a lot of stories about cheating. This client got tired of her husband working long hours, watching television at night, never wanting to spend time with her, and always being too tired to have sex. So she found someone who would spend time with her and have sex with her. She is sticking with the husband, however, because he makes a lot of money. That also seems to be pretty common.

7:20 PM: I really don't care who anyone sleeps with as long as they are properly groomed.

7:30 PM: When this woman told me her husband calls her a "fat cunt," it was hard to know what to say. When she told me that her son called her the same thing, you'd think it would be time to make a change in your life. But when she believes her husband is so much better than his own dad, you know she'll never leave. You see, her father-in-law would make his wife sleep on the kitchen floor when she had her period. She felt fortunate that she didn't have to do that. Not all of my stories are funny, but they are real. I can't make this shit up.

It has been a long day. Time to go home and have a glass of red wine...or two.

10:00 AM: My first client of the day was gay. I don't wax many gay people and I have yet to figure out why. This girl told me she was really nervous about having me see her naked. I always assumed that a lesbian would be more comfortable undressed in front of another woman. She said she was petrified. It turns out she felt very self-conscious in front of me. After several visits, she admitted that she thought I was pretty and wondered if my husband and I were swingers.

10:15 AM: I did a woman who works at my kids' doctor's office. Since I wax women from all over town, it is not uncommon for me to see a client in public from time to time. Finally, this particular secretary got the nerve to get a wax. When I went to the office a few months later, it occurred to me that she hadn't been back. So I asked her what she thought of her wax. She thought that having no pubic hair was great. But she had a real problem. She didn't like the way it felt to have no rectal hair. She told me that she didn't like the way it felt when she farted.

10:30 AM: I had to fight with this one. I am not that big of a woman and I am also not a fan of the WWF. Getting waxed should not be a contact sport. But many times a day, it is. The Battle of the Brazilian may sound fun and kinky to you, but it's a bitch on my body. I am often sore from waxing women whom I am forced to tangle with and hold down their legs in order to get at their parts effectively. This one has locked her legs together. I've given her the option to quit, but she really wanted it done. OK, so if you want me to finish, why are you fighting me? I can't even tell you how badly I wanted to scream, "If you really want it done, open your fucking legs!"

10:45 AM: My next client has had some great stories for me, because she leads a much different life than most people. It was Christmas time and I asked her what she got her husband. She said

101

an Xbox. So then I furthered the conversation by asking what she might get. She told me she asked him for three inches of foam. Huh? It appears she has a small attic with foam on the floor and she wanted more padding to make it more comfortable. I asked her what else was in her attic. She said pillows. I commented that it sounded like a good place for an orgy. She said that was exactly what the area was used for. She had been married seven years and had an open marriage. She liked both men and women and her husband was fine with it. She had a boyfriend for two years who gave her money for spending on herself. That is why she was able to come to me. The boyfriend also gave her husband money. I think that was very generous of him. And it gets even better. The boyfriend had a roommate who dated her husband. In fact, he lived next door to her. So the two women would pass in the night to fuck each other's guys. It's good to have options.

10:58 AM: I told you sex was a big topic in the salon. I have learned a lot over the years.

11:00 AM: The next client got breast implants. Her husband really wanted her to get them and wanted them big. She was tall and slender with a solid D cup. Now that she had these beautiful new breasts, she was getting more attention from other men and it pissed her husband off. Although she was fairly ambivalent about getting her new boobs, her husband had really wanted them. The problem was that now he was psycho jealous every time they went in public and other men would look at her. I'm surprised he let me touch her vagina.

11:15 AM: Although genital piercings are common and I am not surprised when I see them, they are a fun topic to talk about. This college girl said it was the best thing she ever did. She said not only did it intensify her orgasms when she had sex, she would find herself "cumming" by just walking up a flight of stairs. She never took an elevator.

11:30 AM: The next client was a very large black woman who had such a deeply set pair of inner lips that I didn't even notice she had a piercing until it was almost too late. Her hair was so long and dense, I have to admit that I was slapping the wax on aimlessly just trying to get to the Promised Land. Thank God a part of the silver ring caught the light just in the nick of time.

11:45 AM: I wasn't sure what to say to this client. How would you respond to a woman who says that her husband won't have sex with her but loves to whack off to Internet porn?

I have another client who was in severe debt because of her husband's obsession with buying porn on the Internet. She divorced him and basically had to start over.

12:00 PM: This woman is married and has two kids. She got up one morning and went into the bathroom to pee. While she was sitting there, she noticed her husband's wallet lying on the bathroom counter. She had been married about fifteen years. For some reason, she felt compelled to look through his wallet. There were love letters from another woman in there. The letters were explicit about their sexual encounters. There were also credit card receipts from a few local hotels that they had stayed at. When I asked her what she did, she said she stood up, turned around, and threw up.

I had another woman would had a similar experience. One night, she woke up around midnight because her cell phone was ringing. When she answered it, nobody responded. It appears she got butt-dialed from her husband while he was away on business. What she heard changed her life. She listened to him being straddled by another woman. It was graphic and there was no mistaking what she was listening to. When I asked her what she did, she said she went to the bathroom and threw up.

12:15 PM: The next client also has a sad story. She has four children and a drunk husband. Life was difficult but she continued to plug along. She had to. She had four kids. I'll never forget her because she had this nervous habit of pulling her eyelashes out. I could always tell when things were bad at home because she would come in with fake eyelashes on. One night, her husband got in a huge bar fight and got the absolute living shit beaten out of him. He spent a long time in the hospital. Although his limbs were able to heal, his head had been beaten so badly, he was left brain-damaged. She tried to bring him home but his behavior was too erratic and unsafe with the kids there. She had to kick him out of the house, which may seem cruel, but his behavior was so terrifying that she couldn't endanger her children. This story was really sad and I don't know what else happened after that because she couldn't afford to come to the salon anymore. I do know that one of her boys also pulled his eyelashes out.

12:30 PM: Once in awhile, I take a break from waxing and perform other services at the salon. During a facial, I noticed that the client had TMJ. It is pretty easy to recognize while giving a facial because the jaw tends to click when you massage the face at the jaw line. In fact, it is surprising how many women have problems with their jaws. Too much clenching, I guess. Anyway, when I asked her how bad her jaw pain was, she told me that something really embarrassing had recently happened. One of her biggest complaints about having TMJ was the annoyance of having her jaw lock. Not only was it painful, it was often difficult for her to unlock it. While she was giving a very well endowed gentleman a blowjob, her jaw locked around his member and she couldn't release her mouth from his penis. In fact, she had to wait until he went flaccid before she could extricate her mouth from him. As I remember, it didn't take long for her to release her grip because she was causing him so much pain with her tight grip; he was able to shrink up fairly quickly. Whether in the facial, nail, hair, or wax room, every discussion seems to be sex-related.

1:15 PM: A woman in her mid-twenties came in with a pretty serious problem. She had been with a man for two or three years and was even living with him for a while. They had a falling out and she left him for a few months. During that time she confided in me that their sex life wasn't very good. In fact, after sex, she'd go to another room to finish by herself. During their separation, she was actually excited by the idea of having more fulfilling sexual encounters with other men. That never happened, though. She felt guilty and decided to go back to him and give it another try. This time the sex was a little better because he was trying harder and so was she. But she had a real dilemma. Can she spend the rest of her life with a man with an unusually small penis? It shouldn't be a deal breaker, but for some women it is. Her fear was that at some point she would end up cheating on him because she wasn't satisfied that way. But there is also the side of her that feels terribly guilty for even thinking that way. What kind of person judges another on the size of their penis?

It isn't the first time I have met women who have broken up with their men because of the very same reason. I recently read an article about a woman who was worried she was going to hell because she broke up with her boyfriend because he had a small cock. It seems shallow, but it means a lot to a lot of women. But don't worry, gentlemen, there are enough small women in this world that couldn't handle a well-endowed man and you would be a perfect fit for them.

1:30 PM: There is a lot of penis talk in the salon. And it isn't confined to the private wax rooms but in the hair and nail rooms as well. It has to be expected since mostly women occupy salons. After giving this girl a brow wax, she showed me a text her man sent her. It was a picture of her boyfriend's penis totally erect next to a bottle of beer. Light beer, actually. And for the record, it was a very large, good-looking penis.

1:45 PM: When I told my next client that I just saw a picture of a penis standing side-by-side of a beer bottle, she told me she had something cool on her phone as well. She had dancing strippers. When the men took their pants off, they danced around with the most beautifully built bodies and hugely erect penises. It was very entertaining.

2:00 PM: This white girl is dating this Hispanic guy that she doesn't really like. What she does like about him is his really big cock.

2:10 PM: The next appointment is also a penis story. When the client undressed, I noticed a plum-sized skin infection on the inside of her thigh. I was afraid to touch her because I didn't know what kind of infection it was. She told me she got it from a man with an unusually large penis. I asked her to elaborate. She said he liked to shave his entire pubic area. He was a large black man with really coarse hair. It appears that when they had sex, the rubbing caused such severe chafing that she got an infection. In fact, she was on topical and oral antibiotics for one of the nastiest skin infections that I had ever seen.

2:15 PM: Speaking of penises...a girl came in with the most interesting tattoo I have ever seen. Over the years, I have seen thousands of tattoos on just about every square inch of the human body. This tattoo stands out as the absolutely most interesting one I have ever seen and I couldn't believe where she had it put. It was in her cleavage. It was a tattoo of an erect penis coming out of a banana peel with a cum shot pouring out of the tip of it. She was a teenager and I was surprised that anyone would have a tattoo put in such a visible spot, especially considering what it was. She seemed to think that it was in a place that was pretty well hidden. I couldn't imagine any girl letting her parents know about having a tattoo in the middle of her breasts. I asked her what her mom would think about it. She told me that her mom went with her and dared her to do it.

I really have seen some awesome tattoos during my career. I met two women who have had cats faces tattooed where the pubic hair is supposed to be with the whiskers draping into the lip area. The one girl walked into the wax room and asked me if I wanted to see her pussy. She meowed at me before lifting up her skirt to show me her tattoo. It was easy enough to see since she didn't have underwear on. She only had me wax her bikini a few times because she hated seeing any hair on her tattoo, so she decided to continue shaving the area. The hair muted the tattoo and she didn't want anything distracting her cat when she wanted to meow or hiss at someone.

2:30 PM: While I was waxing the next woman, I noticed some redness above her belly button. She lifted her shirt up so I could see what it was. It was a fairly anatomically correct tattoo of a heart with a crack in the middle of it that had been put between her breasts. It was quite large. When I asked her about it, she told me she had a broken heart.

One girl had a tattoo of an arrow on the front of her bikini area that pointed straight down to her vagina. I think that her man needed direction.

2:45 PM: My next client is an animal lover. The pubic area is amazingly smooth and soft when first waxed. I like to tease people and tell them that they'll just want to touch the area because it so incredibly soft. When you shave, it may be soft for a short while, but when the hair grows back, it tends to be prickly. And prickly tends to itch and cause a lot of discomfort. So this is one important reason women prefer waxing. Probably the most amusing description of the way that area feels is when this woman said that her puss felt like a horse's muzzle. I am not a horse fan, but I will take her word that the nose of a horse is incredibly soft. And, for the record, soft is, oh, so sensuous!

3:00 PM: There is also a tremendous amount of talk about vibrators in the salon. This girl had a lipstick case that was actually a vibrator. That takes putting on makeup to a whole new level. I guess lipstick can go on either set of lips.

Vibrators are important to my clients, especially when they are having sex by themselves. I've had women tell me about the different men and other bizarre things they fantasize about when they masturbate. The Rabbit is probably one of the most prized possessions in the average woman's lingerie drawer. The Wand seems to be pretty popular as well. There are women who have much more satisfying relationships with their vibrators than with their partners. There are battery-operated vibrators. Many vibrators plug into outlets. There are even vibrators that can get wet and be used in the shower or tub. There are others that plug in the lighter of your car. Any way, vibrators are popular. Unfortunately, many women tell me that they don't have sex with their partners on a regular basis or at all, so their vibrators are a good alternative. Some of the most satisfying sex can be when a woman has intercourse while using a vibrator. No matter why a woman needs her vibrator, it is an important part of her life and men need to be open-minded about the relationship their girl has with her vibrator. This is just another random thought from my advice column that lives in my head and that I would love to write. Watch out Dr. Ruth. Here comes Dr. M.E.

3:10 PM: I continued the vibrator talk with the next client. She told me that she couldn't use her vibrator because her hair was too long. At first, her proclamation didn't make sense. She told me her hair was so long that it got tangled in the vibrator and pulled her hair when she tried to use it. That is when she knew it was time to come in and see me. Once I made her bald, I knew she would have a satisfying night.

Another woman told me that when she went to masturbate, she had so much hair between her legs that she felt so dirty that she didn't bother to finish. So, I ask you, are we obsessed with pubic hair or what!

3:15 PM: There are women in other parts of our salon getting things done as well. A woman came into the salon for a pedicure and manicure for her birthday. After we finished the service and went to cash her out, she asked me to go into her purse and get out her wallet. She brought a sixty-four--ounce drink into the salon. I thought it was a soda. It wasn't. By the time she finished getting her nails and feet done, she was trashed. So when I reached into her purse to get out her wallet, I pulled out a tan dildo. I was shocked and dropped it back into her purse, because it is pretty gross to touch another person's vibrator. She thought it was the funniest thing ever and couldn't stop laughing.

3:30 PM: My next client loved porn. Some couples need to add some spice to their relationships because their sex life has gotten stale or boring. For some, the answer is pornography. That has been an interesting topic in the salon. So far my data has found that some people like the soft porn stuff that shows good-looking people doing fairly normal stuff. This client just broke up with a guy who only liked the mild type of porn and she preferred it raunchier. Well, that isn't that the only reason she broke up with him. He liked to do it once, quickly, and then put a tissue over his member to clean it off. And that was it. She calls him "the tissue guy." It's hard for me to not laugh whenever she talks about the tissue guy. There are times that it is hard to get certain images out of your head.

Some like to watch the nasty shit that they are too afraid to do. Some like to watch the nasty stuff because it gives them ideas. And there are so many middle-aged women engaging in some crazy S&M activities that I get embarrassed by some of the bondage stories. The nipple clamps, handcuffs, whips, chains, butt plugs, and mysterious toys, to name a few. A forty-something lady with a sixty-something man has hours of erotic, somewhat painful sex. She has never been happier in her life. She met him online. She tears up when she talks about him because she has found her soul mate. I have cried with her because she is so happy. He has made her feel truly loved for the first time in her life. And I would be remiss if I didn't mention the fully equipped dungeon in his basement.

Another woman met a very wealthy married man online who was looking for someone who was into S&M. I'm not sure if his wife wasn't into it or it was more exciting having an extramarital affair or maybe a combination of the two. Some men don't like doing certain sexual activities with the mother of their children, you know. Just watch *The Sopranos* sometimes. This client has been tied down, beaten, asphyxiated, cut with knives, and the list goes on. He has gone so far as to wrap rope so tightly around her breasts that she ended up severely bruised around them. I guess every session ends with some kind of mark left on her body. The world is full of possibilities.

Ever since *Fifty Shades of Grey* became popular, our clients have shared even more stories and experiences with us. There are countless women having an absolute blast in the bedroom. And it is really cool to know that my work on these women make their sex lives even better.

3:45 PM: I'm taking a break and had a flashback. The stories are continuous and occur in every room of the salon. When I was doing nails, there weren't many topics that were taboo in that room, either. One of the discussions was whether or not you let your kids play with guns. It can be quite a controversial discussion, even at a salon. It is a discussion that happened during a series of nail services even before

110

Mark and I started our family. One mom said she really didn't want her son playing with toy guns but when he ripped the heads off of all of his sister's Barbie dolls so he could pretend their bodies were weapons, she caved. Some mothers told me their boys substituted bananas. Other children used sticks. Kids can be very creative. None of these stories were as interesting as the mom who was adamant about her son not playing with toy guns until he discovered an imaginative alternative. He figured out that if he pulled at his penis, it would become hard. Then he would stick it out of his pants and shoot people with it. Now is that creative or what?

When I told this story to one of my clients, she was able to construct another scenario. What happens when the boy starts pulling at his penis enough that things do start shooting out of it?

4:00 PM: Time to wax a man's eyebrows. We have very loyal clients at Mark & M.E. that have been coming to us for years, and this man is one of them. Today, I am reminded of a funny scenario that happened with him a few years ago. When I turned forty, I had breast enhancement surgery. I had wanted it for years and am so happy with the results; I wonder why I waited so long. One day I was giving this man a manicure, and he couldn't stop staring at my chest. Finally, he got up the nerve to ask me if I had gotten my boobs done. I told him that I had gotten them done more than two years before and was surprised he didn't notice. He was absolutely drooling over my breasts, which cracked me up because I had known he was gay for years, and there was definitely no doubt about his sexual preference. He informed me that gay men love women's breasts and if it was okay with me, he really wanted to touch them. So I let him just pat the top of them gently. No big deal. A few minutes later, my husband walked into the room, and I told him that my client loved my new boobs, and that I let him touch them. Mark just laughed and then the two of them discussed how beautiful they were. I guess

111

the moral of the story is that we treat our clients like family and would have it no other way.

4:15 PM: This woman had very long, black pubic hair. When she lifted her leg up and I ripped the first section in this position, she said, "Oh shit, I think I just peed on you." I looked down to see dripping hair and replied, "yep, you sure did."

4:30 PM: Three women came into the room together. A very large, pregnant woman got on the table. She couldn't reach her leg around her belly so I rested it on my back. That's when she yelled, "M.E., you a skinny bitch and when you wax that part, my leg is going to whip you across the room." She had her friend hold her leg for me.

5:00 PM: This woman says fuck, fuck, fuck through the entire service.

5:15 PM: This fifty something client told me that her husband said I am very thorough. I try to be.

5:30 PM: This appointment is with a man who is getting his back waxed. We were talking about my book and some of the gross things in the hygeine chapter. He told me that he got a yeast infection in his mouth from going down on a girl. Now, that is gross.

5:45 PM: This client is a friend of mine who brings tequila with her to her appointments. She does two shots and I do one. What a great way to end my day!

Women are great. They love to talk. They love to gossip. My days are filled with so much laughter. The confessions and the stories are endless. And the best part of my day is all the crazy shit people tell me.

Now He Can Lick Me...

Who would have thought that the life of a Brazilian wax technician could be so interesting or that I could have so much to say on the topic? Even though I've discussed many of the reasons women want to be bald, I think the number-one reason is for sex. Women feel empowered and more confident. Even more important, sex is more satisfying.

When I first started waxing, I couldn't have imagined writing this kind of book. Brazilians weren't that popular. And talking about them was taboo. Now Brazilian waxing is a household term. The popularity of the Brazilian wax has changed my life.

When a woman lets down her inhibitions, life can be so much fun. I am inundated with new stories every day I walk into the salon. The obscenities. The confessions. The hysteria. The drama. Women and waxing are a great topic.

So, take your panties off and let me introduce you to the wonderful world of The Happy Hoo-Ha. When I finish, you can proudly say that now he can lick you, too...

CPSIA information can be obtained at www.ICGtesting.com
Printed in the USA
BVOW02s2147210916

462935BV00001B/7/P